Finding running shoes that fit well

You're never going to get comfortable running if you don't find shoes that fit well. When you find a pair of shoes that you like, see if they meet these criteria:

- ✔ You should be able to wiggle your toes in the *toe box,* or tip of the shoe.
- ✔ Your foot should feel snug in the heel, and there should be no slipping sensation.
- ✔ You should have reasonable flexibility in the forefoot/toe area. (Try bending the shoe slightly with your hand.)
- ✔ The shoe should fit snugly across the top of the foot, but it shouldn't have a straitjacket feel, either. The tongue of the shoe should be padded enough to prevent the shoe laces from irritating, or cutting into, the top of your foot.
- ✔ If the shoes feel stiff, clunky, or simply generally uncomfortable during a test run, don't rationalize that they need to be broken in.

Rules for running safely

Most running safety rules are just common sense, but many runners violate them every day, so we're including them here just to make sure that you can't say we didn't warn you:

- ✔ Don't wear headsets.
- ✔ Run against traffic. A bicycle is considered a vehicle, so it is subject to the same laws as cars and trucks. Cyclists ride with traffic; runners run against.
- ✔ If you run at night, make yourself visible. Wear light-colored clothing and invest a few dollars in a reflective vest.
- ✔ Don't challenge cars to a race. If you and a car are both approaching an intersection, stop and let the car go first.
- ✔ Beware of stopped cars waiting to make a right turn. Stop and wait until they make the turn, or run behind them.
- ✔ Run with others. This may be the easiest way to avoid problems altogether.
- ✔ Avoid running alone in unpopulated, unfamiliar areas and stay away from trails surrounded by heavy brush.
- ✔ Do not wear jewelry. But do carry identification or write your name, phone number, and blood type on the inside sole of your running shoe.
- ✔ Always trust your intuition. If you're unsure about a person or a place, avoid it.
- ✔ Carry a noisemaker or get training in self-defense and the use of pepper spray.

Running For Dummies®

Easy ways to avoid injury

You can greatly reduce the risk for injury if you follow this advice:

- Stay well hydrated. Muscles in a well-hydrated body are less prone to cramping or straining.

- After you've logged 300 to 500 miles on a pair of running shoes, buy new ones.

- Don't run in super-light racing shoes (under 7 ounces) that offer minimal support, especially if you land heavily. Consider light trainers (9 or 10 ounces) as a more supportive alternative.

- Don't run in your basketball or tennis sneakers and don't play hoops or smash backhands in your running shoes!

- Run as much as you can on forgiving surfaces, such as cinder and dirt paths or closely-cropped, flat grass.

- Complement your running with a flexibility and strength-building program.

- Don't try to train through the subtle, little injuries. If you ignore a small injury, it will likely get worse.

- Always warm up and cool down.

- When mapping out your yearly training program, factor in some downtime. Runners need some periods of reduced training, cross-training, or even complete rest from running.

Are you overtraining?

You might be overtraining if . . .

- Your morning pulse rate is suddenly elevated. Suppose that your normal resting pulse rate is 60 to 64. But for the better part of a week, it's up around 70 or 71.

- Your performances in both races and hard workouts have leveled off, or even fallen, even though you feel like you are putting a 100-percent effort into your running.

- Normally an energetic runner, you inexplicably don't feel like running for days at a time.

- At the start of a training run, your legs feel "dead," or they're always sore and tight.

- Your sleeping patterns get weird. Maybe you can't sleep at night (even though you are training harder than ever), but you feel like you can barely stay awake in the late afternoon.

- Every cold or flu bug that comes around wants to reside in *your* body and hang around for a while.

- Normally a nice, happy person, you suddenly have a short fuse and a long face.

- You find yourself sneaking out the door at 11 p.m. for a 3-mile run. It's the end of the week and you already have in 47 miles, but you think that 50 will look a lot better in your training log entry.

...For Dummies: Bestselling Book Series for Beginners

Flo-Jo Memorial Community Empowerment Foundation

The Flo-Jo Memorial Community Empowerment Foundation is committed to MAKING DREAMS COME TRUE for the youth of America and all over the world. The foundation will provide young people with the necessary financial, emotional, and educational support they need to achieve their goals, promote self-esteem and social interaction, all while involving family and friends in the process.

Founded upon the principles of Florence Griffith Joyner and Al Joyner, who believe that all childeren deserve the opportunity to follow their dreams and make them a reality, the Flo-Jo Memorial Community Empowerment Foundation challenges us all to

Dare to

Reach

Excel

Aim high

Make it happen!

For more information about the Flo-Jo Memorial Community Empowerment Foundati on, call toll free 1-877-58 FLO JO (1-877-583-5656). You can also write to

Flo-Jo Memorial Community Empowerment Foundation
26522 La Alameda, Suite 270
Mission Viejo, CA 92691

To make a difference and support the Flo-Jo Memorial Community Empowerment Foundation, you can wire funds to

Northern Trust Bank of California N.A.
355 South Grand Ave., Suite 100
Los Angeles, CA 90071
Credit Account: 50904094
Routing Number: 12242173

Praise for Running For Dummies

"The toughest distance in running is always the first steps out the door and down the driveway. . . . But *Running For Dummies* does just about everything for you short of lacing up your shoes. A GREAT guide for the beginning runner . . . It provides easy-to-understand information and is filled with insightful tips. It's a must-read for the new runner."
— John "The Penguin" Bingham,
Runner's World columnist

"Running is the simplest of sports and fitness activities, and this book keeps it that way, while at the same time thoroughly covering the basics of pursuing a lifetime of healthy, productive running. This book is certain to inspire runners of all backgrounds to pursue their goals and give them the tools to achieve them."
— Gordon Bakoulis, Editor-in-Chief, *Running Times*

"Florence Griffith Joyner will be remembered among America's greatest Olympians and she will be recalled with the legends, like Wilma Rudolph and Babe Didrikson Zaharias."
— Bill Hybl, USOC President

™

References for the Rest of Us!™

RUNNING FOR DUMMIES®

**by Florence Griffith Joyner
and John Hanc**

Foreword by Jackie Joyner-Kersee

IDG
BOOKS
WORLDWIDE

IDG Books Worldwide, Inc.
An International Data Group Company

Foster City, CA ♦ Chicago, IL ♦ Indianapolis, IN ♦ New York, NY

Running For Dummies®

Published by
IDG Books Worldwide, Inc.
An International Data Group Company
919 E. Hillsdale Blvd.
Suite 400
Foster City, CA 94404
www.idgbooks.com (IDG Books Worldwide Web site)
www.dummies.com (Dummies Press Web site)

Library of Congress Catalog Card No.: 98-88808

ISBN: 0-7645-5096-9

Printed in the United States of America

10 9 8 7 6 5 4 3 2 1

1B/RV/QR/ZZ/IN

Distributed in the United States by IDG Books Worldwide, Inc.

Distributed by Macmillan Canada for Canada; by Transworld Publishers Limited in the United Kingdom; by IDG Norge Books for Norway; by IDG Sweden Books for Sweden; by Woodslane Pty. Ltd. for Australia; by Woodslane (NZ) Ltd. for New Zealand; by Addison Wesley Longman Singapore Pte Ltd. for Singapore, Malaysia, Thailand, and Indonesia; by Norma Comunicaciones S.A. for Colombia; by Intersoft for South Africa; by International Thomson Publishing for Germany, Austria and Switzerland; by Distribuidora Cuspide for Argentina; by Livraria Cultura for Brazil; by Ediciencia S.A. for Ecuador; by Ediciones ZETA S.C.R. Ltda. for Peru; by WS Computer Publishing Corporation, Inc., for the Philippines; by Contemporanea de Ediciones for Venezuela; by Express Computer Distributors for the Caribbean and West Indies; by Micronesia Media Distributor, Inc. for Micronesia; by Grupo Editorial Norma S.A. for Guatemala; by Chips Computadoras S.A. de C.V. for Mexico; by Editorial Norma de Panama S.A. for Panama; by Wouters Import for Belgium; by American Bookshops for Finland. Authorized Sales Agent: Anthony Rudkin Associates for the Middle East and North Africa.

For general information on IDG Books Worldwide's books in the U.S., please call our Consumer Customer Service department at 800-762-2974. For reseller information, including discounts and premium sales, please call our Reseller Customer Service department at 800-434-3422.

For information on where to purchase IDG Books Worldwide's books outside the U.S., please contact our International Sales department at 317-596-5530 or fax 317-596-5692.

For information on foreign language translations, please contact our Foreign & Subsidiary Rights department at 650-655-3021 or fax 650-655-3281.

For sales inquiries and special prices for bulk quantities, please contact our Sales department at 650-655-3200 or write to the address above.

For information on using IDG Books Worldwide's books in the classroom or for ordering examination copies, please contact our Educational Sales department at 800-434-2086 or fax 317-596-5499.

For press review copies, author interviews, or other publicity information, please contact our Public Relations department at 650-655-3000 or fax 650-655-3299.

For authorization to photocopy items for corporate, personal, or educational use, please contact Copyright Clearance Center, 222 Rosewood Drive, Danvers, MA 01923, or fax 978-750-4470.

About the Authors

Florence Griffith Joyner

Florence Griffith Joyner truly serves as a modern emblem of the American Dream. Born in Los Angeles and raised in Watts, she was the seventh of 11 children raised by a divorced mother who instilled in her children the values of independence and individualism. Though one brother practiced martial arts and another football, Florence was unique among the Griffith family in her athletic prowess, competing with her brothers on their own demanding terms.

Florence began running at the age of 7 under the auspices of the Sugar Ray Robinson Youth Foundation. By adolescence, she had become an accomplished long jumper and one of the top runners at Jordan High School in Los Angeles, where she regularly defeated boys her own age. Joyner did not seclude herself in athletics, however. A straight-A student, she enrolled as a business major at Cal State-Northridge before earning a scholarship to UCLA where she studied psychology. Joyner's track and field skills blossomed at UCLA and she first qualified for the Olympic trials in 1980, finishing fourth in the 200-meter and making the finals in the 100-meter event. In 1981, she was the American Record Holder in the World Cup 4x100 meter relay. In 1982 and 1983, she was the NCAA Collegiate Champion in the 200-meter and 400-meter events. In 1983, Florence became a member on the first World Championship Team held in Helsinki, Finland, where she finished fourth in the 200-meter event.

In 1984, Joyner earned the silver medal in the 200-meter track event at the Los Angeles Summer Olympics. Though she considered it a great honor to finish second, Joyner set her sights on the next Olympic Games, intent on taking home the gold. In the intervening years, she sharpened her competitive edge by winning the Champion's crown in the 100-meter sprint at the 1985 Mobile Grand Prix, the gold (4x100 meter relay) and silver (200-meter) medals at the 1987 World Championship.

1988 proved a year of fruition for Florence Griffith Joyner, the first American woman to win four medals, three gold and one silver, in one Olympic year. The Queen of Seoul, Joyner opened a floodgate of honors in the wake of her performance: The Sullivan Award, to the most outstanding American female or male athlete, The U.S. Olympic Committee's Sportswoman of the Year, *Track and Field* Magazine's Athlete of the Year, Associated Press Sportswoman of the Year, UPI Sportswoman of the Year, Jesse Owens Outstanding Track and Field Athlete, Jesse Owens International Award, and Tass News Agency's Sports Personality of the Year.

Recognized by her brightly colored, often one-legged outfits and intricately painted fingernails, Joyner captured the affection of the world with a rare combination of speed, grace, and beauty. Her still standing World Record times in the 100- and 200-meter events have rightly earned her the title "World's Fastest Woman."

Honors from around the world have recognized not only her athletic ability, but her new status as a role model. Joyner also won accolades from institutions (Harvard) and publications (*Essence, McCalls, Track & Field News, Life,* and *People*). Even television networks have bestowed upon her awards such as, The Nickelodeon Kid Choice Award, The People's Choice Award, The Positive Image Award from Women at Work, and The Golden Camera Award from the German Television Industry. Recipient of a Distinguished Service Award from the United Negro College Fund, Joyner was always in demand as a spokeswoman for such worldwide concerns as Project Eco-School (a resource center for environmental education), The American Cancer Society, and The Multiple Sclerosis Foundation.

In 1993, Joyner was chosen by President Clinton to become the first woman ever to hold the Chair of the President's Council on Physical Fitness and Sports, replacing Arnold Schwarzenegger.

Flo-Jo and her husband Al Joyner encourage goal-setting through the Florence Griffith Joyner Youth Foundation, a nonprofit organization helping America's youth set and follow their dreams. The Foundation provides youth with the necessary financial, emotional, and educational support in achieving their expressed goals: promoting self-esteem and social interaction while involving family and friends in the process.

John Hanc

John Hanc is the running and fitness writer for *Newsday*. Hanc is the author of two previous books on running, both published by The Lyons Press, *The Essential Runner* and *The Essential Marathoner.*

His articles on running and fitness have appeared in publications such as *Runners World, Playboy, Reader's Digest, Men's Health, Running Times,* and *Men's Fitness.* He is also an associate professor of communication arts at the New York Institute of Technology in Old Westbury, New York. Hanc has run 11 marathons, most recently the Prague International Marathon in May, 1998. In addition to running, Hanc enjoys weight lifting, cycling, and pushing a stroller with his 3-year-old son in it. He lives in Farmingdale, New York with his wife, the aforementioned 3-year-old, and about seven pairs of running shoes.

ABOUT IDG BOOKS WORLDWIDE

Welcome to the world of IDG Books Worldwide.

IDG Books Worldwide, Inc., is a subsidiary of International Data Group, the world's largest publisher of computer-related information and the leading global provider of information services on information technology. IDG was founded more than 30 years ago by Patrick J. McGovern and now employs more than 9,000 people worldwide. IDG publishes more than 290 computer publications in over 75 countries. More than 90 million people read one or more IDG publications each month.

Launched in 1990, IDG Books Worldwide is today the #1 publisher of best-selling computer books in the United States. We are proud to have received eight awards from the Computer Press Association in recognition of editorial excellence and three from Computer Currents' First Annual Readers' Choice Awards. Our best-selling ...For Dummies® series has more than 50 million copies in print with translations in 31 languages. IDG Books Worldwide, through a joint venture with IDG's Hi-Tech Beijing, became the first U.S. publisher to publish a computer book in the People's Republic of China. In record time, IDG Books Worldwide has become the first choice for millions of readers around the world who want to learn how to better manage their businesses.

Our mission is simple: Every one of our books is designed to bring extra value and skill-building instructions to the reader. Our books are written by experts who understand and care about our readers. The knowledge base of our editorial staff comes from years of experience in publishing, education, and journalism — experience we use to produce books to carry us into the new millennium. In short, we care about books, so we attract the best people. We devote special attention to details such as audience, interior design, use of icons, and illustrations. And because we use an efficient process of authoring, editing, and desktop publishing our books electronically, we can spend more time ensuring superior content and less time on the technicalities of making books.

You can count on our commitment to deliver high-quality books at competitive prices on topics you want to read about. At IDG Books Worldwide, we continue in the IDG tradition of delivering quality for more than 30 years. You'll find no better book on a subject than one from IDG Books Worldwide.

IDG BOOKS WORLDWIDE

John J. Kilcullen
John Kilcullen
Chairman and CEO
IDG Books Worldwide, Inc.

Steven Berkowitz
Steven Berkowitz
President and Publisher
IDG Books Worldwide, Inc.

VIII WINNER

Eighth Annual Computer Press Awards ≥ 1992

IX WINNER

Ninth Annual Computer Press Awards ≥ 1993

X WINNER

Tenth Annual Computer Press Awards ≥ 1994

XI WINNER

Eleventh Annual Computer Press Awards ≥ 1995

IDG is the world's leading IT media, research and exposition company. Founded, in 1964, IDG had 1997 revenues of $2.05 billion and has more than 9,000 employees worldwide. IDG offers the widest range of media options that reach IT buyers in 75 countries representing 95% of worldwide IT spending. IDG's diverse product and services portfolio spans six key areas including print publishing, online publishing, expositions and conferences, market research, education and training, and global marketing services. More than 90 million people read one or more of IDG's 290 magazines and newspapers, including IDG's leading global brands — Computerworld, PC World, Network World, Macworld and the Channel World family of publications. IDG Books Worldwide is one of the fastest-growing computer book publishers in the world, with more than 700 titles in 36 languages. The "...For Dummies®" series alone has more than 50 million copies in print. IDG offers online users the largest network of technology-specific Web sites around the world through IDG.net (http://www.idg.net), which comprises more than 225 targeted Web sites in 55 countries worldwide. International Data Corporation (IDC) is the world's largest provider of information technology data, analysis and consulting, with research centers in over 41 countries and more than 400 research analysts worldwide. IDG World Expo is a leading producer of more than 168 globally branded conferences and expositions in 35 countries including E3 (Electronic Entertainment Expo), Macworld Expo, ComNet, Windows World Expo, ICE (Internet Commerce Expo), Agenda, DEMO, and Spotlight. IDG's training subsidiary, ExecuTrain, is the world's largest computer training company, with more than 230 locations worldwide and 785 training courses. IDG Marketing Services helps industry-leading IT companies build international brand recognition by developing global integrated marketing programs via IDG's print, online and exposition products worldwide. Further information about the company can be found at www.idg.com.   10/8/98

Authors' Acknowledgments

From Al Joyner:

This book is the work of a true champion who was blessed with the unique gift to empower others with her insight and motivation, and through her words and good deeds. I am forever grateful to so many people for helping make Florence's dream of writing a book come true. This list can only acknowledge those who were involved in the preparation of this book, and even with that qualification, I'm afraid I've left some people out, but here goes:

To Stacy Collins, who ran with the baton to John Kilcullen, with confidence and undying faith in me to carry on Flo-Jo's conviction, belief, devotion, dedication, and dream that *Running For Dummies* would inspire and help others to make their own dreams come true. To John Hanc, Mark Will-Weber, Tim Gallan, and Tina Sims for putting Florence's thoughts, feelings, and emotions about running down on paper to share with the world. And to the entire staff at IDG Books, for their understanding and their never-give-up attitude.

To my loving sister, Jackie Joyner-Kersee, for just being you. To Mary Ruth Joyner, for being a special gift that we received from God, to help keep me focused on what's really important in life, which is to help others to achieve their dreams.

Thanks to Jill Smoller, of ICM, for making the call to IDG Books, Bobby Kersee for making me stay on the right track, and Andre Phillips, 1988 Olympic Gold Medalist, for making me laugh about the good times. To all my friends, neighbors, and colleagues who believed in me throughout the years: Nu Skin International (Blake Rodney, President; Steve Lund, Vice President; Jason Chaffertz; and the entire Nu Skin and IDN staff); Saucony (John Fisher, CEO; Art Rogers, President; and Nancy Ohnuma); David Brownstein of Writer & Artist; Elite International Sports Marketing; Final Kick Marketing Group; and JT Communications.

To all the fans all over the world who share my lasting happiness, hurt, and pain for the love of my life, Flo-Jo, I thank you.

From John Hanc:

Big-time thanks to our technical editors for their contributions, especially my buddy Mark Will-Weber, senior editor at *Runner's World* magazine; Mona Shangold, M.D.; coach Marty Stern; and my good friend and running doc, Thomas Scandalis, D.O.

We also want to thank all of the other coaches, exercise physiologists and runners who generously shared their knowledge and expertise with us, for various parts of this book. They include Jeff Galloway, Owen Anderson, Ph.D., Wayne Westcott, Ph.D., Bob Anderson, Henley Gabeau of the Road Runners Club of America, Ryan Lamppa of USA Track and Field's Road Running Information Center, and Richard Miller of The Gym Source in Manhattan.

Also thanks to Al and Flo, acquisitions editor Stacy Collins, and our project editor Tim Gallan for his patience and coolness under fire; to Nick Lyons, Doug Hynes, Raleigh Mayer, Lee R. Schreiber, Judy Cartwright, and Ginger Rothe for their guidance and support of my involvement in this project; to all our training partners and running buddies; to my Mom for her constant encouragement and my wife Donna and son Andrew for putting up with their Dummy dad.

One last note:
This book was largely complete on September 21, 1998, the day that Flo-Jo died. She was my co-author, and she was enthusiastic and excited about this project. At first, IDG Books and I weren't sure if it would be right to publish this book without her. But her husband, Olympian Al Joyner, decided we should.

You can read more about Flo and her legacy in the special tribute section that has been included in this book. But for the purposes of your own running, you should know this: Although Flo became famous as a sprinter, she genuinely loved distance running, and she wanted to share that love with others. Nothing would make her happier than to know that someone, someone like you, took their first steps as a result of this book. May you get the same joy and satisfaction on the run as she did.

Publisher's Acknowledgments

We're proud of this book; please register your comments through our IDG Books Worldwide Online Registration Form located at `http://my2cents.dummies.com`.

Some of the people who helped bring this book to market include the following:

Acquisitions and Editorial

Senior Project Editor: Tim Gallan

Acquisitions Editor: Stacy Collins

Copy Editor: Tina Sims

Technical Editors: Marty Stern; Mona Shagold, M.D.; Thomas Scandalis, D.O.

Editorial Manager: Leah Cameron

Editorial Coordinator: Maureen Kelly

Acquisitions Coordinator: Karen Young

Editorial Assistant: Donna Love

Production

Project Coordinator: E. Shawn Aylsworth

Layout and Graphics: Daniel Alexander, Linda M. Boyer, Angela F. Hunckler, Anna Rohrer, Brent Savage, Kate Snell

Proofreaders: Kelli Botta, Vickie Broyles, Toni Settle, Janet M. Withers

Indexer: Steve Rath

Photographer: Michael Neveux

General and Administrative

IDG Books Worldwide, Inc.: John Kilcullen, CEO; Steven Berkowitz, President and Publisher

IDG Books Technology Publishing: Brenda McLaughlin, Senior Vice President and Group Publisher

Dummies Technology Press and Dummies Editorial: Diane Graves Steele, Vice President and Associate Publisher; Mary Bednarek, Director of Acquisitions and Product Development; Kristin A. Cocks, Editorial Director

Dummies Trade Press: Kathleen A. Welton, Vice President and Publisher; Kevin Thornton, Acquisitions Manager

IDG Books Production for Dummies Press: Michael R. Britton, Vice President of Production and Creative Services; Cindy L. Phipps, Manager of Project Coordination, Production Proofreading, and Indexing; Kathie S. Schutte, Supervisor of Page Layout; Shelley Lea, Supervisor of Graphics and Design; Debbie J. Gates, Production Systems Specialist; Robert Springer, Supervisor of Proofreading; Debbie Stailey, Special Projects Coordinator; Tony Augsburger, Supervisor of Reprints and Bluelines

Dummies Packaging and Book Design: Patty Page, Manager, Promotions Marketing

◆

The publisher would like to give special thanks to Patrick J. McGovern, without whom this book would not have been possible.

◆

Contents at a Glance

Cartoons at a Glance

By Rich Tennant

Fax: 978-546-7747 • **E-mail:** the5wave@tiac.net

Table of Contents

Foreword

●●●

*I*n my heart there will always flow the legacy of Florence Griffith Joyner, my sister-in-law and the person to whom I dedicate the following reflections.

Florence Griffith Joyner's contributions to society will undoubtedly last forever. Rarely do individuals possess the kind of strength, stability, and substance that took her from the ghetto of south-central Los Angeles to the White House in Washington, D.C. Moreover, her ability to visualize success and bring it to fruition, I believe, made her a remarkable person. She was loved by many, and she touched more lives than I can count.

Never once did I see her frown on people who weren't successful. Instead, she shared her achievement with everyone she encountered, encouraging them to follow their dreams. Embraced by many as a Christian, entrepreneur, and humanitarian, Florence, known as the "Fastest Woman in the World," was rare. Her accomplishment as a world-class runner sparked an interest in track and field for girls all over the world.

Florence's exploits on the athletic field generated so much attention that girls of all ages were striving to be the next Flo-Jo. It was Florence's wish, however, that these girls work hard, be committed to their own endeavors, and be better than she was. Every little girl she touched or encouraged will remember her as a giving person, someone who gave of herself and made sure that others had smiles on their faces. Those qualities were rarely seen in the newspaper and rarely shared in articles.

It's sad that a woman of her character is no longer here to challenge us to continue to strive for what our hearts desire. All Florence had were her dreams, and making them real was her strength. Now that spirit lives on in her work. In *Running For Dummies,* Florence shares her expertise on running posthumously. The book was one of many dreams come true, and she looked forward to meeting fans as she traveled the book tour with her husband, Al.

Florence was a loving wife and mother who will be missed eternally, a woman who transcended her sport and captivated the world with her beauty and grace. Yet through it all, she never forgot how she got here. I hope we never forget Flo-Jo, Dee Dee, Florence Griffith Joyner: a legend, a remarkable person. Her spirit will live forever.

Jackie Joyner-Kersee

Introduction

● ●

*T*here was a time when most folks would have thought that anybody running for any reason other than to catch a bus was a dummy.

How things have changed. In 1998, over 32 million Americans went for a run. Hometown 5-Ks are as common as bake sales, and big city marathons cause as much excitement as political conventions. Now, an entire industry has emerged out of what essentially began when one visionary coach — the legendary Bill Bowerman of Oregon — poured rubber into his wife's waffle iron to create a new kind of shoe: a running shoe.

Bowerman and all the great coaches of talented runners over the decades deserve our respect. But the running movement is not about talent or running fast. It's about getting out and doing the best you can, and reaping a harvest of benefits, in the process.

For that, let's give credit to Dr. Kenneth Cooper, whose 1968 book *Aerobics* turned a light on the now-established link between exercise and prevention of heart disease. Give credit to Frank Shorter — a Yale law student who won the 1972 Olympic marathon and inspired a generation of upper middle-class professionals to lace up their shoes. Give credit to Bill Rodgers, the popular Boston Marathon champ, and to Dr. George Sheehan, the author and running-philosopher; to Kathrine Switzer and Nina Kuscsik, who started the women's running movement in the 1960s; and to Joan Benoit, whose victory in the first Olympic women's marathon in 1984 probably did for women's running what Shorter's did a decade earlier. Let's also give credit to Fred Lebow, who turned the New York City Marathon into the Greatest Show on Earth, and to Grete Waitz, who became its brightest star and most gracious ambassador. Give credit to Oprah Winfrey, who used her own show as a vehicle for showing others that running a marathon wasn't just for super-athletes. And yes, give credit to Jim Fixx, whose *Complete Book of Running* in 1977 helped ignite the running boom of that decade; but whose death of a heart attack in 1984 reminded us that running alone is not a panacea. (Something that all of us associated with this book were reminded of all over again in September of 1998.)

All of these individuals deserve a salute for transforming running from a sport for a few talented elites into a mass movement. But above all, give credit to yourself.

Yes, you. Because by picking up this book you're taking the first step on a great journey. The 1990s have seen a second running boom, one composed not just of college-educated, upper-middle-class men, but of folks of both sexes, and of all ages and abilities. They're running for fitness, for fun, and for friendship; and they're likely to keep it up right into the next century.

Come on. Join them.

How to Use This Book

If you're a beginner, we recommend that you start by reading Parts I and II, where we show you how to get started. If you're already running, you may want to go right to Part III, where we show you how to move up to the next level. You can even use our book to focus on one specific area of your training. Want to run a marathon? Check out Chapter 14. Need to buy a new pair of running shoes? We'll tell you what to look for in Chapter 5. Looking for a weight training regimen that can help your running? Turn to Chapter 17. And so on.

How This Book Is Organized

This book consists of five parts, each of which contains chapters that cover related topics.

Part I: Run, Baby, Run

In this part of the book, we tell you a little bit about the new running boom that you're about to become a part of. We tell you why people run; why so many (including us) seem to love it so much; and why so many medical experts applaud it and encourage it. We give you a brief and simple explanation of what happens to your body when you run, and how to fuel it properly for running. We also help you choose the most important and (some might say) only vital piece of equipment you need to run: shoes. Then we take you through your first steps as a runner — and show you to stay motivated and consistent.

Part II: Basic Training

We'd like you to think of *Running For Dummies* as your own personal coach. And this is where we blow the whistle and get to work. (Don't worry, it's satisfying work, and it can be fun, too.) In this section, we show you proper running form, discuss the value of hills in your training, and cover some other basics, like how to warm up properly and how to run safely and continue running through even the toughest weather conditions.

Part III: The Competitive Edge

So now you're fit. Let's put it to the test: This section shows you how to take your first steps towards racing a local 5-K. We tell you the kind of training you need to do to run your fastest. And then, if you're ready for a real challenge, we show you how to train for and complete your first marathon.

Part IV: Fine-Tuning

Most physicians recognize the value of running in promoting cardiovascular health and will applaud your efforts. The exceptions are the orthopedic surgeons and podiatrists who've had to repair the damaged knees and feet of runners who've run too much for too long. You can avoid injuries and mental fatigue by training intelligently. In this section, we show you how. We also offer some special tips for women, seniors, and youngsters on the run.

Part V: The Part of Tens

If you only have ten minutes, here's a way this book can help you right away: Check out our tips on how to sharpen your mental edge. Or peruse our lists of ten beautiful races, ten great races for women, and ten perfect marathons for first-timers.

The Running Log

Don't forget the running log at the back of the book. You can use it to record your progress as you develop a training program.

Icons Used in This Book

As you flip through this book, you'll see little pictures next to chunks of text. We call these pictures *icons*. Here's what they mean:

We flag pertinent tricks, secrets, and general good advice with this icon.

To warn you of the potential for injury and other dangers, we use this icon.

Running, like many sports, seems to have a language all its own. We use this icon when we explain the jargon.

When presenting little bits of running trivia, we use this icon.

People have all kinds of strange notions when it comes to running, fitness, and nutrition. When we're debunking myths, we use this icon.

This icon flags anecdotes and words of wisdom from Florence.

Where to Go from Here

Take a look at the Table of Contents or the Index and find a topic that interests you. This book is a reference, not a tutorial, so feel free to skip around and read whatever section catches your fancy. Or you can read the book from cover to cover, which would make us happy too.

Part I
Run, Baby, Run

The 5th Wave   By Rich Tennant

"I think you're in fine health to begin running as an exercise. I would, however, do all I could to avoid getting shin splints."

In this part . . .

This part is a great starting point for the beginning runner. We give you some background on the latest trends in running, we tell you why running is good for you, we show you how to get started, and we even help you with buying the right shoes.

Chapter 1

The Second Running Boom

- -

In This Chapter

▶ The new running boom

▶ Running for your health

▶ Running for a cause

- -

*1*t's the end of the 20th century, and we're on the run — literally.

A new running boom is sweeping the country — and reverberating across the rest of the world. It's different from the running boom of the 1970s. That, you may recall, started back in 1972, when Frank Shorter's unexpected gold medal in the Olympic marathon inspired a generation of middle- and upper-class men to lace up their sneakers and hit the local track.

Shorter was an articulate, Yale-educated lawyer and a somewhat unlikely athletic hero. Lawyers, bankers, accountants, and stockbrokers took heart in his great achievement. The men in these professions (few women ran in those days) were urged on by their doctors, who were beginning to take notice of the research showing the health benefits of activities like running. Soon, these runners donned sweatbands and polyester jogging suits and began taking to the streets and sidewalks of America.

The runners in the first running boom were competitive but one-dimensional. They just ran and ran. No cross training. No stretching. No weight lifting. None of the things that we runners now know we must do to stay healthy. They created an industry — athletic footwear — and provided a new windfall for podiatrists and orthopedic surgeons. They transformed events like the New York City and Boston marathons from relatively small races for serious athletes only into mass-participation sporting events.

The New York City Marathon grew from 55 finishers in 1970 to 12,512 in 1980! Today, it's up to over 30,000.

Give the original running boomers credit. Although they may have overdone it, they helped fuel a national revival in fitness, one that eventually brought us step aerobics, stairclimbing machines, and a health club on every corner.

How the Second Running Boom Is Different

The new running boom that you are helping to sustain is different. It's more diverse, for one thing. All kinds of people are running as this second running boom continues. Senior citizens, youngsters, physically challenged individuals, people of all classes and ethnic backgrounds, and perhaps most significantly, women have joined the ranks of runners.

Over 33 million Americans went for a run in 1996, making it the fourth most popular fitness activity in America. That's an increase of about 53 percent since 1987. Of these, 5 million are frequent runners — defined as folks who run two or more times per week.

According to the USA Track and Field Road Running Information Center in California, the percentage of women finishers in U.S. road races has been climbing steadily over the last decade: up to 32 percent of all finishers in 1997. Women now account for almost half of the finishers of all 5-K (3.1 miles) races nationwide and for 28 percent of all marathon (26.2 miles) finishers.

In round numbers, that's 112,000 female marathon finishers in 1996 as opposed to 15,000 in 1980, the height of the first running boom. In other words, eight times as many women are running marathons today.

In the country's largest road race, the Bay to Breakers 15-K in San Francisco, history was made last year when, for the first time in the event's 86-year history, more than half the field was female: That's 30,000 women out of just under 60,000 total finishers.

Why are so many people running? One survey of regular runners found these answers:

- 95 percent say they run to keep in shape.
- 92 percent say they like the mental benefits.
- 76 percent say they do it to relieve stress.
- 70 percent say they run for weight control.
- 36 percent like to compete.

Women and running: We've come a long way

In the bad old days, women weren't allowed to participate in some of the running events where men raced because men thought women weren't physically capable of enduring long runs. As a matter of fact, for a long time, women weren't allowed to run any distance farther than the 800 meters.

One female athlete in particular, Kathrine Switzer, inspired many women to get involved in running. Switzer signed up for the Boston Marathon in 1967 under the name K. Switzer. A race official found out that she was a woman and tried to prevent her from running; he even tried to rip her number right off her chest. A group of people came to Switzer's aid and prevented the official from getting to her, and Switzer did finish running the marathon.

Women were not allowed to run in the Boston Marathon officially until 1972. It took a heroic act from Kathrine Switzer to make men realize that women can indeed complete a marathon. The doors were opened for millions of other female athletes who were just waiting for such an opportunity.

Running for the Health of It

The most basic reason to run is to improve and maintain your health. We talk a little bit more about just how running helps you, what it does to and for your body, in the next chapter. For a moment, let's back up to the difference between that first running boom of the 1970s and the current one. Those people in the second running boom have a different attitude towards running than their hardcore predecessors in the 1970s. The folks in this second running boom, folks like you, are more likely to see running as part of a healthy lifestyle. Today's runners make running only one part of a routine that also includes perhaps weight training, stretching, proper nutrition, and other sports or activities.

The runners of the '90s also tend to be less concerned with performance. The average finish time in marathons has gotten slower and slower over the past 15 years, for both men and women. The average runner took 3 hours, 32 minutes, 17 seconds to cover 26.2 miles in 1980. Today, the average time is 3 hours, 54 minutes. For women, the median time went from 4 hours, 3 minutes, to 4 hours, 15 minutes.

These runners aren't as concerned about competition and performance. Competition can certainly still make running fun, and many fierce competitors certainly are out there. But the runners of today are less concerned with PRs (that's running lingo for "personal records") than with the enjoyment, fulfillment, and sense of achievement that come with regular running. In short, they're running with a healthier attitude.

Maybe runners today are taking their time because they're enjoying it more, or at least enjoying the company of other runners. You may think of running as a lonely, solitary activity. And for some people it is; in fact, that's precisely why they run. They want to get away from it all and escape from the computer, the fax, and the phones. But for so many others, running is a chance to socialize, and running with people, instead of away from them, is a great way to pass the time while you're running. You chat, you compare notes, you talk about everything and anything under the sun as the miles click along. Training groups and running clubs have flourished because of the companionship that running can offer.

Sports psychologists say that one of the best ways to start and stick with a running program is to find somebody to do it with you. So forget that myth about the "loneliness of the long-distance runner." Running actually can be a very sociable sport. Just ask any of the dozens of men and women who propose or get married at the finish lines or along the routes of marathons every year!

Running for a Cause

Another reason that today's runners are hitting the roads concerns people, but not necessarily people they know. Women in particular like to run in fund-raising events for special causes. Two of the largest new running and racing programs in the country, for example, are about helping others.

The Race for the Cure, a series of 5-K running events, is now held in 86 cities around the country and has helped raised millions of dollars to fund breast cancer research and promote prevention. The Leukemia Society of America's Team in Training is an equally successful program. Participants in this marathon training program raise money for victims of leukemia and other diseases while they train to run and complete a marathon, usually in some exciting location, like London, Vancouver, or Hawaii.

Chapter 2
What Running Can Do for You

"*W*hy do I run?" That was the question posed by a major athletic footwear marketer in a recent TV commercial. The ad showed runners on the track and the roads, pounding, racing, gasping, grimacing. At the end of the spot, the question was answered: "To win."

Boy, was that commercial off the mark, at least when it comes to the average runner. The average runner doesn't run to win races or medals. That doesn't mean we don't run to compete — most runners are constantly trying to improve, to go a little farther, a little faster than last time. From the moment you take your first steps in your running program, you'll probably want to keep improving. At some point, you may decide to enter a race, competing against the clock or runners of similar ability.

But "winning" is an elusive if not irrelevant goal to most runners. It's the physical, mental, and social reasons described in this chapter that provide ample rewards for most of us. The good feeling we get from running. The sense of confidence and achievement. No, we don't run to win. We run because it makes us feel like winners, no matter how slow or how fast we go.

Why should you start running?

Think about it a moment, even as you're reading this book about running. Why should you bother? Why not just sit back down on the couch? Why not choose another activity? Why not walk, swim, cycle, or take step aerobics classes? They're all fine ways to exercise. Why make the effort — yes, especially when you get started, running is an effort — to begin a running program? Simple. Because running can change your life — more effectively and with less expense and less equipment than any other activity.

We're not lying or exaggerating about the dramatic effect that running can have in your life. Over the years, we've met and heard about hundreds of people whose lives have literally been transformed by running. Non-runners may not believe how beneficial running can be, but it's true. Running has rocked people's lives — improving the way they look, they way they feel, they way they think, and the way they look at life. Runners value the good feeling and sense of confidence and achievement that they get from running. People run because running makes them feel like winners, no matter how slow or how fast they go. Runners will tell you that running has enhanced their lives in many ways. And it can do the same for you, too. What follows are some of the physical, mental, and social benefits that you can expect if you start running.

The Physical Rewards of Running

Running is so good for you in so many ways. That's not to say that you can't run too much. You can. But a sensible running program — the kind that we show you how to follow — is one of the most effective, convenient, and cheapest ways to get all the wonderful benefits of exercise.

Running can help you lose weight

People can lose 10, 20, 50, or 100 pounds or more through running. (Probably one of the most famous celebrities who lost weight on a running program is Oprah Winfrey, who shed 70 pounds.) Runners who lose weight and keep it off — which diet alone can't always do — gain a new sense of self and self-esteem.

Running burns a ton of calories — about 100 calories per mile. You can burn about the same amount by walking; the only difference is that it takes less time to run a mile than to walk a mile, so in the same time, you'll burn more because you'll cover a greater distance than most walkers.

When I started running again after the birth of my daughter, I had over 50 pounds to lose. What helped me greatly was constant positive reinforcement. I didn't think of myself as a fat runner because I knew that such negative thinking wasn't going to help me lose the weight. So I gave myself words of encouragement as I trained, focusing on where I needed to be and not where I was at. I believe that positive input puts out positive results!

Running is good for your heart

Why do athletes in other sports run as part of their conditioning regimens? Why are recruits in boot camp ordered to get up at dawn and run 5 miles every morning? Because running is the most basic form of exercise. Because this is the fundamental route to fitness; to improve endurance, to "get in shape." Runners tend to have greater stamina for other sports and for everything else in their lives.

Running has profound and positive effects on the most important muscle in the body: your heart. A runner's heart is one strong muscle:

- A runner's heart is more efficient: It pumps more blood, less often.
- A runner's heart beats less at rest and at work (as observed by the lower-than-average pulse rates of most runners).
- A runner's heart is less stressed — meaning that it needs less energy to function.

Running and exercise are linked to increased levels of HDLs (the so-called good cholesterol) and lower levels of LDLs (the bad cholesterol) and triglycerides, leading to lower total cholesterol levels.

There is an important relationship among running, insulin, and blood pressure. A runner's body has a decreased need for insulin, which generally means you're less likely to suffer from hypertension.

Running is part of a healthy lifestyle

Although running can do a lot of good things for your body, running alone can't ensure a healthy heart. Genetics, diet, and other factors play a role, as well. If you survive on a diet of cheeseburgers and fries and drink a six-pack of beer a night, running 3 miles a day isn't likely to prevent your arteries from getting clogged. Runners do have heart problems, like anyone else, but the incidence is far less than in the general population. What's more, runners tend to adopt healthy lifestyles. You may find that your eating, drinking, and lifestyle habits will fall into step with your running.

We've even known people who have quit smoking through running. When they started one habit, they couldn't continue the other. And the good feelings that accompany running are apparently powerful enough to break even the addictive hold of nicotine, at least among some people.

Moderation is the key to a healthy lifestyle, not total deprivation. Recognize your weaknesses and try not to overindulge in the foods you love. If you want to eat a hamburger with french fries, go ahead. Just don't do it every day. You'll probably improve your attitude and commitment to your program if you treat yourself occasionally for being disciplined with your running.

Sprinting versus running

Pant, pant, pant, gasp, gasp, gasp. These sounds are some people's idea of what running must be. Some people assume that you must run as fast as you can, to the point of exhaustion. Sprinting, as Flo can tell you, has its benefits. But the kind of running we're talking about, distance running, is not about pain, not about pushing beyond your limits, not about pushing hard, especially at the beginning. The benefits of running come not from running hard, but from running at a comfortable pace. (We show you how to find that pace in Chapter 4.)

A run should be enjoyed. Pushing yourself too much too soon can become discouraging, and you may find yourself looking for other means of exercise after a while.

Running can help you live longer

The value of a regular, aerobic exercise program in helping to protect against many diseases and in prolonging life is now beyond question. Study after study has shown that people who exercise regularly live longer, healthier lives. The U.S. Surgeon General, the American Heart Association, and the Centers for Disease Control and Prevention recommend regular exercise to help improve the quality and longevity of life. Running is not the only exercise that can deliver these benefits. But no exercise delivers those benefits as inexpensively and efficiently as running.

To add to the well-known health benefits of running, a recent study shows that people who exercise regularly are less likely to develop gallstones and gall bladder disease than those who don't. Although a number of different kinds of exercises can help lower the risk, the exercises that worked the best were vigorous activities, such as — you guessed it — running. In fact, the researchers concluded that running 2 to 3 hours a week can reduce your risk of gallstone disease by 20 to 40 percent.

The Mental Rewards of Running

Research has shown that running is almost as good for your head as it is for your heart. Individuals on a regular running program have been shown to have increased confidence and motivation, less anxiety, lower rates of depression; more pep and vigor, and, generally, a greater sense of well-being. The following are some of the mental benefits of running.

What's a runner's high?

Endorphins are brain chemicals, natural opiates, commonly thought of as being the source of the *runner's high* — the sense of exhilaration that many runners report feeling during or after a run. But scientists disagree as to whether or not endorphins are really the reason for this feeling. In one study, runners were given an endorphin-blocking drug, and they still felt the high! The researchers concluded that the exercise high was something more subjective, a feeling triggered by the pace, the rhythm, or perhaps even just the sensations of being outdoors. The point is, whether or not it's chemical, running gives many people a natural, pleasant buzz.

Running reduces stress

Running frees you from the things that stress you out. Running can get you out of the office or the house. Running gets you away from the fax, the phone, and the computer and into a quieter place. Running is so popular with business executives and professionals because it gives them time away from the office or the classroom — time that's theirs and theirs alone. Spending time outdoors, in the fresh air, and allowing the body to move the way it was meant to move can help you better deal with life's daily stresses.

My mother has given birth to 11 children, and if anyone knows what it's like to live with stress, she certainly does. She says that exercise, whether walking or running, makes her feel young and helps her forget about the stresses in her life. She enjoys exercising and doesn't allow anything to prevent her from being outdoors to smell the flowers and hear the birds chirping.

Running can boost creativity

Okay, this may sound a little flighty, but running can be like magic. It's hard not to feel good about yourself when you're running. You become energized, excited, and focused.

Running has helped people solve complex problems, imagine successful businesses, write poetry, prepare for final exams, and work through issues and challenges facing them in their lives. Runners often find that their exercise time is when they do their most creative, productive thinking. The creative juices can really start flowing when runners are immersed in the wonderful feeling that accompanies the rhythm of running.

Young experts sound off about why they run

Listen to the wise words of youngsters, ages 9 to 16, who were asked to write essays on what makes them run. Excerpts of these essays were reprinted in a recent issue of *Footnotes,* the magazine of the Road Runners Club of America. Here are some of the kids' comments:

✔ "I run to have fun competing with others. I run to get things off my mind. I run to be proud of myself."

✔ "Running is a fun sport, and it's good for you. Running is also important because it's included in other sports. Another reason that I run is because every course is different. Some courses are hard, and some are easier. Some have pretty scenery, and some do not. Different courses challenge you in different ways. These characteristics set running aside from other sports. This is why I run."

✔ "I run because it makes me feel good about myself."

✔ "I see that running is making a positive impact in my life, and I'm going to continue doing it."

✔ "I run because if I run, I stay fit and healthy. If I didn't run, I would be as fat as the Nutty Professor. And also, if you run, you can do almost anything! It doesn't matter how old you are to run! Running is an all-year sport! Even if I don't win, I feel good because I finished! That's why I run!"

When you come up a great idea, maybe the next big thing, while running, write it down when you stop. You may even want to keep a log of what you've thought about while running and maybe go over some of your great ideas on subsequent runs.

Social Rewards of Running

Running does more than help improve your physical and mental health. It can improve your social life, too. People make best friends and meet their husbands, wives, boyfriends, girlfriends, and their entire social circles, all through running. Runners find that like-minded folks — men and women who enjoy being outside, enjoy being healthy, and enjoy the sheer joy of movement — are the best kind of company.

When I was training for the 1988 Seoul Olympics, Al Joyner, who was my boyfriend, tagged along on my runs — short runs, long runs, and even circles at the training track in the gym. Now what's funny about these dates is that Al hated to run! But because he wanted to spend time with me and get to know me better, he made the sacrifice. Little did I know he was plotting to make me his wife. So you never know what can happen during a jog around the block or a 5-mile run.

Running Is Good for Your Wallet

Few exercises do as little damage to your pocketbook as running. You can run at no cost no matter where you are. You don't need an expensive health club membership if you want to be a runner. When you're on vacation, you can take a run on the beach. If you're going away on business, don't forget to pack your running shorts so that you can explore the streets around the hotel. (Check with the concierge to get a map and to make sure that the neighborhood is safe.)

Running demands none of the equipment of sports such as cycling or skiing. If running is your sport, you don't have to drive to a special place to exercise, as you would if you wanted to swim or play tennis. Plus, you don't have to pay admission to a pool or hefty fees for court time. You don't need to buy any big, expensive apparatus or travel to a certain location. You can simply lace up your shoes and go for a run wherever you happen to be — in the city, in the country, along the shore, up and down hills, or through fields. You can run on streets, on trails, on a track, or even indoors on a treadmill.

Outside of a modest initial expenditure on a decent pair of shoes and proper clothing, you won't have to spend a dime to run.

Running is a great investment. Your principal is low. Your rate of return is enormous, and it keeps growing every year. And there are no hidden charges, unless you count an occasional blister.

Chapter 3

A Body in Motion

• •

In This Chapter

▶ How your body develops energy for running

▶ The role of your circulatory and respiratory systems

▶ Why running is good for your bones

▶ Why running is as natural as breathing

• •

*W*hat happens to your body when you run? What are the changes (the *adaptations,* as the sports docs like to call it) that occur when you put one foot in front of the other and start to move. And what are the long-term effects? That's what this chapter is all about: a look at running from head to toe.

Running: An Inside Look

When you start to run, the cortex — the part of the brain that monitors the motions of your body — gets the message and swings into action. It tells the heart to snap to and start working harder. The heart does its work, pumping faster in order to supply nutrients to your legs. Your lungs pull harder, taking in more oxygen, which is also transported to the legs and the rest of the body through the bloodstream.

Meanwhile, the body's energy manufacturing centers also begin to hum with activity — providing no less than three different types of fuel to the body:

✔ The first energy source is through carbohydrates, found in the cells of your muscles.

✔ After you've run for a little while, a new source arrives from the liver: glycogen, which is converted into blood sugar and then delivered through the bloodstream.

✔ A third source that kicks in — primarily in longer distance running — is fat. We're not talking about obesity or weight loss here, but simply fat as fuel. For more on this topic, see Chapter 6.

Running on Empty

So you're running along and this remarkable fueling and refueling system is working in a high gear. What's to keep you from going on and on forever? Well, a number of factors. The first is a sensation you may already be familiar with: It's called *fatigue*. It's what happens when you exercise at an intensity that you can't sustain or begin to run out of fuel.

Lactic acid build-up

Beginning runners — who are asking these systems to work in this way for the first time — often feel the effects of *lactic acid,* which causes, among other things, the soreness you might feel in your legs after your first few runs.

Lactic acid is a chemical substance, a normal byproduct of a body in motion. Generally, the greater the intensity of your exercise, the higher the amount of lactic acid your body produces. When you reach a certain point, and there's too much of it for your body to handle, lactic acid can cause soreness, fatigue, and nausea. But here's the trick: That point can be raised by exercising. In other words, the fitter you are, the longer it will take your body to reach that point (called *the anaerobic threshold* because it's the point at which the exercise is too intense for your body to depend on its oxygen delivery system to meet its needs).

What does all this mean for a beginning runner? It means that you need to start slowly, yes, but you do need to make an effort, you do need to push at times, a little beyond the point of comfort. Never beyond the point of pain, severe shortness of breath, dizziness, or nausea (which are also symptoms of overheating, by the way). If you have those symptoms, stop. But remember: A little soreness and fatigue after a workout isn't necessarily bad. These symptoms really mean that you're doing what it takes to get your body into shape.

Body temperature

Another element of fatigue involves body temperature. If your body gets too hot, you're going to have to stop — and if it gets really hot, the whole system could collapse, which is what happens when you have heat distress. (More about that in Chapter 10.)

Running: The Heart of the Matter

Running is good for your heart. Now that doesn't mean runners are guaranteed never, ever to have heart attacks, or that running alone will prevent you from having any kind of heart problems. But a regular running regimen will help your heart and your entire cardiovascular system in many ways:

✔ Running keeps your arteries elastic, which helps keep your blood pressure low. Blood can't flow as easily through stiff arteries — and that's when the pressure rises.

✔ Your heart is a muscle, and like any muscle, it benefits from exercise. Running does it better than almost any other activity. Running helps keep the heart pumping stronger and more efficiently. It also keeps the coronary arteries open and working at full capacity, so that the heart can pump at a greater volume.

✔ All the heart pumping, blood flowing and muscle-moving action of running requires plenty of oxygen. Running forces your lungs to work to their full potential.

That's what you want, and that's what running delivers. A body in motion, a body with the throttle open, a body that gets the exercise it craves. Remember the saying, "Use it, or lose it." A tragically high number of people are losing the strength and vitality in their bodies, the power of their hearts and lungs, simply because they do nothing to challenge them.

Running provides that challenge — one that your body will welcome and thrive on.

I was diagnosed with a heart murmur when I was 14 years old, and it scared me a great deal. The doctors told me that I could exercise as strenuously as I desired, and that made me feel good. Through running and proper diet, I have been taking care of my body ever since. If you have any kind of pre-existing heart condition, you will want to get clearance from your doctor before running. But don't be scared, and do not use something like that as an excuse to not even consider an exercise program. Let your physician make that decision with you. But chances are, he or she will encourage you to exercise, just as mine did.

Fine-Tuning the Machine

Suffice it to say, running initiates a complex biochemical process. If you had to consciously coordinate it all, forget it.

But the good news is that the more you run, the more efficiently these systems begin to operate. It's like anything. Your body has a learning curve, too. The body of a fit, experienced runner is much better at utilizing energy than a beginner, which also means that a fit runner is better able to withstand the stress of running.

Here's a simple example: The average person's heart beats about 72 times per minute. The heart of a fit runner beats at almost half that rate — in the low 40s or even the high 30s, in the case of some elite runners. Why? Because their hearts are stronger and more efficient. What's more, at the same workload, the runner's heart rate and blood pressure are going to be lower than the average person. And when they finish, their heart rates will return to normal far more quickly. In other words, while the average guy is still sucking wind, the runner is breathing comfortably and is probably ready for more! Over time, you'll be able to get to that point, too.

Meanwhile, Back in the Bones

We've talked about the heart and lungs and the body's energy and temperature-regulating systems. But there's another part of the body that works hard during running: Your bones and the connective tissues — ligaments, tendons and muscle — are pumping away, providing the actual power that moves you forward, and functioning like shock absorbers every time you hit the ground.

This is good. Bones need to be stimulated to maintain or increase their density. Running does that. Even the *microtraumas* — the small tears that occur in the muscles through a repetitive exercise like running, can be good, despite the ominous sound of the word. Why? Again, because they provide a stimulus for the muscles to get stronger.

How Much Is Too Much?

All of the positive changes caused by running — increased heart and respiratory efficiency and increased bone density and so forth — will only take place if you give the body the chance to make the changes. To rebuild, restore, refurbish itself for the next run. Which is why it's very important not to run too hard, too far, too often. How much is too much? It's very individual, of course. For example, if you're one of the great Kenyan runners, your biomechanics, your bodyweight, and your oxygen delivery capabilities are perfect for running. So you can make like that TV bunny in the commercials and keep going, and going, and going.

Few of us are blessed with such talents. The average person's body can't usually withstand the rigors of daily running. So it's probably a wise idea to get into the habit of running alternate days, and no more than four or five days per week.

Running: It's in Our Blood

Most of us aren't built to run like the great world-class marathoners. But we are very definitely built for movement. Which is one reason that public health officials have been urging Americans and others to do just that: Get up and move. When people say, "Oh, running is no good for you," we have to laugh. Running no good? Sitting in front of a computer for eight hours or being crammed into the driver's seat of your car during a traffic jam: That's no good.

We humans were designed to run and walk for long distances. "Our ability to move for long distances at sub-maximal speeds is a gift to our species, like language," says ultradistance runner and exercise physiologist, Stu Mittleman. As proof, he cites such examples as the migrations of tribes, armies on the march, and our hunter-gatherer ancestors.

You want to talk about a marathon? The prehistoric migration of people from Asia across the land-bridge that once connected that continent with North America: Now that was a marathon. (And come to think of it, the descendants of those people, who became known as Native Americans, produced — among other things — many fine runners.)

So don't let anyone tell you that running is something unnatural. Sure, there is a point of too much. And no, the body is probably not designed to do a marathon every day. But you were born to run. Maybe not that fast, maybe not that far, maybe not as efficiently as others. But to get up and move, to fire up that entire energy-producing, oxygen-delivering, bone-strengthening process we call running. It's one of the most natural things you can do.

Chapter 4

Your First Steps

*E*nough about why you should run. You know now what it can do for almost every aspect of your life. It's not that hard to get started. And we've got a surefire program that will enable you to make the transition. It's easy to understand, and with just a little discipline and dedication, we'll turn you into a runner before you can say "oxygen debt" (and if you can say that, you're not running hard enough!). Beginning running should be a smooth, gradual, and fun process. So lace up those shoes, and let's get going!

Make an Appointment

Some people say that visiting your doctor for a check-up before you start running is "boilerplate" advice. Others say that if you're young and healthy, you don't need to do it. But we still argue that getting your doctor's approval is a good idea. Certainly, you should see your physician if you're over 35 or have a history of heart problems or any other risk factors, such as smoking, diabetes, or high blood pressure. But even if you have none of these risk factors and are in the pink of health, an annual check-up is still probably a good habit to get into, just like running.

Make the Commitment

One of the first questions that people ask when starting a running program is "When is the best time of day to do it?"

The best time is the time that's best for you. Schedule your running at a time when you know that you will be able to do it. If that means first thing in the morning, great. If it's when you get home from work, terrific. If it's lunchtime, or your child's naptime, or the time you usually spend watching TV or surfing the Net, that's fine, too.

After you've studied your schedule and identified that hour or so that you can set aside for running, stick to it. That time must become your regular time to run. Don't make it a flexible date that you can use for other activities. In fact, you might even consider making an appointment with yourself. Write "5 PM, Thursday: Run" in your calendar or daily planner.

Research shows that people are more likely to stick with an exercise program if they exercise at a consistent time — not willy-nilly, at different times throughout the week — and if they exercise with somebody else. Decide on a time and then perhaps consider trying to find a running partner.

Some of you may be wondering whether it's better to run in the morning or in the evening. Our answer: It doesn't matter — at least for the beginner. There are pros and cons for running at either time of day, but for the beginner, the key issue is to get out and run regularly. In fact, we know of many people who will use the fact that they can't work out in the morning to not run at all because they heard that running in the morning is somehow better than in the evening. Bottom line: Don't worry about that stuff, and don't give yourself any lame excuses not to run.

FLO-JO SAYS

Finding the time

When I was a customer service representative for a bank the year before the 1988 Olympics, I had to make time to run: before I went to work, on my lunch hour, and after work. It was no easy task, but the results were great. Before I started training, I had no idea how I would be able to squeeze in any time to work out, but because I wanted so badly to achieve my goals, I made every sacrifice I could. Sure, there were many occasions when it seemed like I had no time to do anything else but work and train, but I felt that the results would be worth the effort.

I found that working out in the morning helped get me going for the rest of the day, and working out in the afternoons helped relax me from a long day at the office. I won't kid you and suggest that working out can't often seem like a chore, but I will tell you that the benefits far outweigh the sacrifice.

Make a Pact

Although some people start running by themselves, others take the plunge with a friend, spouse, or other family member. Consider the example of Gordon Bakoulis, now the editor-in-chief of *Running Times* magazine.

Gordon (a she, by the way) started running back in college. She was not a scholarship athlete but simply a student looking for a way to get in shape and relieve the stress of grades, classes, and exams. She and a friend made a pact to run together every morning. "It turned out to be a good idea," recalls Gordon. "Because when you woke up at 6:30 and wanted to roll over and go back to sleep, you'd remember that somebody else was standing outside waiting for you. It sort of forces you to do it, because you don't want to let the other person down."

Bakoulis didn't disappoint anyone. She not only stuck with her running through college, but she became one of the best female marathoners in the country. She competed in the U.S. Women's Olympic Marathon Trials in 1992 and 1996. Although Gordon may have more talent than most beginning runners, remember that she started the same way you did by taking the same basic steps.

Meet Your Local Running Club

A running club is a great way to break into the sport and to enhance your enjoyment of it. Contrary to popular belief, these clubs are for runners of all levels and all abilities. In fact, they're often as much about socializing as they are about running. Most clubs hold regular meetings, publish a newsletter, and organize trips to out-of-town races. Clubs can be great fun and a great source of information, inspiration, motivation, training partners, and new friends.

The Road Runners Clubs of America has 620 affiliated clubs. They range in size from a couple dozen members to the 31,000-member-strong New York Road Runners Club. Chances are, there's a club in or near your community. To find one, you can call the RRCA at 703-836-0558. Or you can e-mail the RRCA at office@rrca.org or visit the Web site at http://rrca.org.

The loneliness of the long-distance runner

The solitary, antisocial figure on a long, empty road, enduring unspeakable agony while pondering the meaning of life. That's the common image of the distance runner. And although some runners certainly fit that stereotype, that's really what it is: a stereotype, and a dated one at that. The average runner these days is in it for fitness and fun. And we do have fun. Today's runners tend to be gabbers, socializers, and schmoozers, as evidenced by the hundreds of running clubs that flourish throughout the United States and Canada. Runners tend to travel more in packs than alone, running together and traveling in groups to races, expos, and pasta parties.

Runners have good reasons to be sociable: Having training partners helps the time pass, pushes you to greater heights as a runner, and introduces you to an entire new group of friends. Together, you'll share the road, share the surroundings, share some good stories, and maybe even, if you're like many of today's not-so-lonely long-distance runners, share a pizza or even a beer after the run!

Keep a Logbook

Most serious runners keep a logbook, or training diary, in which they write down information on every workout, sometimes in painstaking detail. You don't have to make this the Captain's Log on the Starship Enterprise ("Star Date 26.2: The Klingons attacked an M class planet in our quadrant while I was tying my shoelace"), but keeping a running record is a good idea. You may want to buy a special training diary that includes useful training advice and inspirational quotes. But your personal training diary doesn't have to be that fancy. Just make a note of the date, the workout, the weather, and how you felt.

A training log is a learning tool; by writing down what you did on a certain date, you're creating a database that can help you progress as a runner. You'll know how far you went the last time so that you can decide how far and how hard you need to go on the next run. Especially for the beginning runner, a training log is also a motivational tool. As you see the progress you've made, you will feel the sense of achievement and be able to see that you're advancing and improving. That's the kind of feeling that can help put a spring in your step during the next workout!

The running log at the back of this book is a great tool to help you record your progress.

On Your Mark, Get Set, Walk . . . Then Run

Just keep in mind the watchwords of a good beginner's running program:

- ✔ Patience
- ✔ Consistency
- ✔ Gradual improvement

You're probably eager to start running, but before you run, you must walk. Walking is a wonderful form of exercise in and of itself, and it's also the way to start a running program.

We're not talking about a window-shopping saunter here. This is brisk, purposeful walking. To paraphrase the words of that famous pedestrian president Harry Truman, walk as if you have someplace to go. Walking conditions the body and prepares it for the greater stresses of running.

Walking versus running?

Walking versus running is the topic of much hot debate today. Some walkers disparage running, warning people that it will ruin their knees (which it won't do, if you train properly). Walkers also often like to point to some studies, mostly funded by walking shoe companies, that show that walking burns more calories than running. The truth is, you burn about the same number of calories with both activities, but walking a mile takes longer than running a mile. So if you run 30 minutes, instead of walking 30 minutes, you'll burn more calories because you're covering more distance.

Running is more challenging and more satisfying than walking. But trying to position walking and running as adversarial or contradictory activities is ridiculous.

First of all, walking is a great way to get fit (and competitive racewalking is as tough as any other endurance sport). Second, running and walking go together in many forms and fashions. Ultradistance runners — those who run farther than the 26.2-mile marathon distance — tend to walk and run. Some marathon training programs emphasize the importance of regular walking breaks. Walking is a good way to warm up before a run. And beginning runners are advised to start a running program by walking.

Now, you could ignore that advice, and go out and run hard for as long as you can. You may feel good at first, but eventually your body will start sending off all kinds of signals designed to get you to stop. Your throat will burn, your chest will heave, and your legs will scream. The next morning, your muscles will be so mad at you that they may try to stop you from getting out of bed.

So be smart, even if you're young and in shape. Walk before you run. How far? Well, that does depend on your age and condition. But generally, we recommend building up to the point when you can walk 45 minutes briskly, nonstop, before you begin to run.

Questions you should ask (and that we'll be happy to answer)

Before you make the transition from walking to running, we want to answer the most basic and commonly asked beginners' questions.

How often should I run?

The short answer is "not every day." Indeed, for all but the very best runners — those people who have built-for-the-long-haul bodies — running seven days a week, week in and week out, is a surefire recipe for injury. Instead, try to shoot for four workouts a week. But don't assume that you don't have to do anything on the other three days. In fact, the U.S. Surgeon General's office recommends that all Americans get 30 minutes of moderate activity every day. That doesn't necessarily mean running 30 minutes a day. You can walk, cycle, or perform household chores or yard work to get in your 30 minutes of activity. For more on running as part of an overall fitness program, see Chapter 16.

How long should I run?

The American College of Sports Medicine defines aerobic exercise as activity that lasts from 20 to 60 minutes. That's a wide span. Forty-five minutes is the so-called gold standard of aerobic exercise. You can benefit from doing a little less or a little more, but many cardiologists agree that 45 minutes is the ideal length of time needed to accrue many of the physiological benefits of aerobic exercise. So although you certainly won't start out by running 45 minutes, ultimately that's a good goal to shoot for.

How hard should I run?

As you make the transition from walking to running, remember this: Running is not sprinting. You should perform your running intervals at a comfortable pace. The best way for a beginner to find the right pace is to use the time-honored *talk test*. If you can comfortably carry on a conversation while you're running — without huffing and puffing — you're in the right training zone. If you can carry a tune — that is, find the breath to sing — you're probably not running hard enough.

You're an exception to our guidelines if you've had heart problems in the past. In that case, your cardiologist will probably have you wear a heart monitor when you start exercising. You can read more about that useful tool in Chapter 5.

Where should I run?

Runners tend to run in one of four places:

- ✔ Tracks
- ✔ Roads
- ✔ Trails
- ✔ Treadmills

Beginning runners should start with the track and then eventually explore the other three options.

The local high school or college oval, which is 400 meters or about a quarter-mile long, offers a measured distance, a good surface, and a closed, safe environment. Also, if you're a bit self-conscious, you can run there and not worry about nosy neighbors getting a glimpse of you in shorts and strange-looking shoes.

So one of the steps to starting a running program is to find a local track. And we do mean local. If it takes you 2 hours to drive to it, that's one more potential excuse to blow off your workout.

Another option is a marked, measured recreational path at a local park. Another possibility is to hop in your car and measure out a mile-long loop in your neighborhood, starting and ending at your door. Make sure that the route follows a road that's well paved and as traffic-free as possible. You want a place where you can concentrate and feel relatively comfortable. This is, after all, where you're going to learn to run.

The walk/run approach: A program to get you going

After you're comfortably able to regularly complete 45 minutes of brisk nonstop walking, you're ready to incorporate a little running into your routine. How little will depend on you. But here's what we recommend:

1. **The day that you're ready to start running, go down to the track and walk four laps.**

   If you don't have access to a track, walk for 16 minutes.

2. **Now try a nice easy jog for one lap, or about 2 to 3 minutes.**

   If one lap is too much, try a half lap.

   Don't worry about speed. Just stay relaxed, maintain a "conversational" pace, and focus on good form (which we discuss in Chapter 7).

3. **Now walk two laps (or about 8 minutes) and jog another lap (about 2 to 3 minutes).**

4. **To finish up, walk four laps, or about 16 minutes.**

That's 3 miles on a quarter-mile track. You've just finished a good 45-minute workout. Try doing that for the next couple exercise sessions. Remember that you should be working out three to four times a week, or every other day. Your body needs 48 hours to adapt to the new workload that you've placed upon it.

As you continue to train (and if you are feeling good), you can increase that ratio of jogging to walking. Try walking for two laps (or about 8 minutes) and then jogging for two laps (or about 6 minutes). Or walk a lap and jog a lap, until you've exercised for about 45 minutes or 3 miles.

It's natural to have some muscle aches when you begin a new exercise program. But any injury that hurts during the walking phase of your early training sessions should not be subjected to running. Check with a doctor who has experience treating runners if you suspect that you have a running-related injury. (Chapter 15 describes the most common running injuries.)

You're on the Run!

Some individuals will be able to run farther distances, sooner, than others. You must let your own body be your guide as you make the transition. But don't try to do too much, too soon. Proceed slowly and err on the side of caution. Your watchwords while working up to a run should be gradual improvement and patience.

Learn a lesson from a health club aerobics instructor we know. She was in shape and could step with the best of them. She didn't have an ounce of fat on her spandex-covered body.

She wanted to start running, so she did just that. She began with a walk/run program, but every time she went out, she added another mile or so of running, far more than we recommend for beginners. Within 2 weeks, she was running almost 6 miles. By the third week, she was complaining about knee pain. That was the end of her running program — at least for a while.

Don't make the same mistake that she did. Proceed gradually from walk to run/walk to running. You may need a few weeks, or even a few months, to get to the point where you can run nonstop for most of those 45 minutes. But with patience and diligence, you'll get to the point where you can run nonstop for 30 minutes, or about 3 miles, depending on your pace. (You also need to allot about 10 minutes of walking to warm up and 5 minutes to cool down.)

At the end of that workout, pat yourself on the back.

You're a runner now, pal.

Chapter 5

Cruising for Shoes and Other Equipment

· ·

In This Chapter

▶ Shopping for shoes

▶ Matching shoes to your feet

▶ Looking for optional equipment

· ·

*A*bebe Bikila of Ethiopia won the 1960 Rome Olympic Marathon through the streets of Rome (the shoe companies *hate* this part!) while running barefoot! And Czech great Emil Zatopek, who won four Olympic gold medals, hammered through training runs in heavy combat boots.

But we mere mortals need a smoother, more comfortable ride: a ride that increases our enjoyment and lessens our injury risk. That's why choosing your shoes is one of the most important aspects of a beginning running program.

Other equipment — stopwatches, heart monitors, and high-tech sunglasses — are all extras. Unlike shoes, you don't *have* to have them, although such items can enhance performance and fun.

Shopping for Shoes

Your chances of landing in a comfortable, quality pair of running shoes greatly increases if you shop at a running specialty shop rather than a huge, multisport center attempting to hawk everything from bowling balls to scuba gear to in-line skates. Employees of most running specialty shops typically are people who run themselves. The best running shops also serve as the center of your local running community and can be a gold mine of information on training, upcoming races, and group fun runs.

Here's one telltale sign of a good running specialty shop: It not only allows you to take the shoes for a 5-minute test run, but it encourages you to do so. If the store doesn't let you test-run in the shoe, don't plunk down your dollars there.

Knowledgeable running store employees will most likely ask you (nicely) the following questions before they try to fit you in a particular shoe:

✔ How much running experience, if any, do you have?

✔ How many miles a week do you run?

✔ What type of surface do you run on?

✔ Do you have any short-term goals for your running program? For example, are you training for an upcoming race? ("Yeah, I'm planning on winning the Boston Marathon next spring.") Or do you simply want to get around the block three or four times a week? ("I want to be able to keep up with the guy who played Norm on *Cheers*.")

The answers to such questions can help the running store people steer you in the right direction.

Shop for your running shoes in the afternoon. Why? Because your feet tend to swell slightly throughout the day, and Rule Number One is to avoid buying shoes that are too small! (Your feet also swell slightly during a training run.) And be sure to wear athletic socks of the same thickness that you'll wear when you run.

Before You Shop

You can speed up and assist in the shoe-choosing process in two ways. First, take the "wet test" (covered in the following section) to determine what kind of foot you have, such as high-arched as opposed to flat. Second, if you tried to run or walk in a relatively recent life, bring in your old shoes. Even if the most vigorous thing you did in them was escort your toy poodle down to the corner mailbox and back, the wear pattern on your shoes may be helpful to the store employees.

Wet test: Tracking your footprints

You don't have to be Sherlock Holmes to learn something from your foot-prints. Wet the bottom of one foot and then step firmly onto a flat surface. (tile — or sand — works). If you have a flat foot, you'll leave a fat, complete footprint. If your footprint appears almost severed in half vertically, so that virtually no print from your arch is visible, then you have a high arch. A so-called normal foot is somewhere in between: The footprint will show about half of the arch. Figure 5-1 shows some wet test footprints.

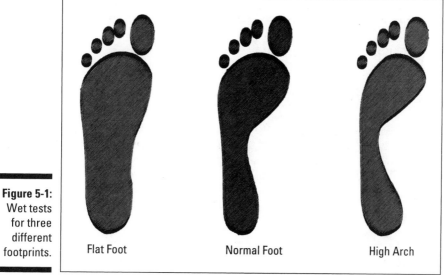

Figure 5-1:
Wet tests for three different footprints.

Flat Foot   Normal Foot   High Arch

Knowing something about what type of foot you have *before* you head to the running shoe store can at least steer you toward a range of models with the specific technology to address your potential problems.

Wear patterns and foot strike

By examining the wear patterns (the places on your shoes worn smooth by repetitive use) of your old shoes, a knowledgeable shoe guru may get some clues about particular models that will fit you best. Reading wear patterns isn't an exact science; one shoe expert admitted that "It's a bit like reading tea leaves." But the more information you start with, the better your chances of getting fitted in a top-rate shoe.

Foot strike is a term that you may hear bantered about in a running shoe shop, as in "Are you a heel striker or a forefoot striker?"

Most runners tend to be *heel strikers,* who land on the outside of the heel and then roll up to push off the ball of the foot and the toes. A few runners are *forefoot strikers* and land more on the ball of the foot.

Wear patterns on shoes can tell a lot about foot strike. A forefoot striker (the wear pattern typically results in a smooth area around the ball of the foot) may need a shoe with plenty of forefoot cushioning. An ultraheavy heel striker requires extra cushioning in the heel.

Figure 5-2 shows the various parts of a typical shoe so that you can identify the areas where you may need extra cushion.

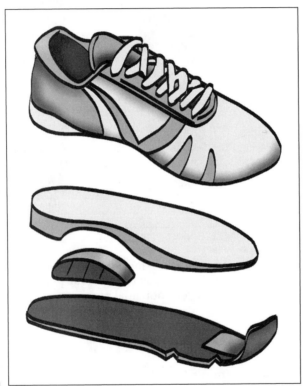

Figure 5-2:
The parts
of a shoe.

Pronation

Inevitably, you will hear the term *pronation* if you're in the company of sports podiatrists, running store staffers, or veteran runners or coaches.

The physical act of running isn't just a case of putting one foot in front of the other; running is a somewhat complex biomechanical process. Most runners (except the forefoot strikers) strike the ground on the outside of the heel. Next, the rest of the foot comes down and rolls slightly inward as it meets the surface. (This down and inward roll rotation is called *pronation*.) Lastly, the heel lifts off the ground as the runner propels himself off the ball of the foot and toes, applying the necessary force to move forward. The repetition of this process makes a person a runner (regardless of speed).

Pronation in itself is not a bad thing because it helps your feet and legs absorb shock. However, excessive pronation — rolling in too much — can cause increased injury risks. That's called *overpronation,* and the answer to it is finding a shoe with good motion-control properties. Runners with flat feet (and those with bowed legs) tend to be prime candidates for overpronation woes.

Runners who overpronate need a "straight" shoe (as opposed to one that curves at the tip) with a firm midsole for motion-control (to prevent the foot from rolling inward too much upon footstrike). (The very bottom of the shoe is called the outsole; the next layer up — the one designed for shock absorption duty — is the shoe's midsole.)

A much less frequent problem is *underpronation.* Although they're a rare breed, underpronators tend to have an inflexible foot (and often a high arch, too), and when they land, their feet don't make much of a rolling-in motion. The result is a lot of pounding force. A runner that lands like a ton of bricks and underpronates definitely requires a shoe with plenty of cushioning to absorb the shock.

Figure 5-3 shows overpronation, underpronation, and a happy medium.

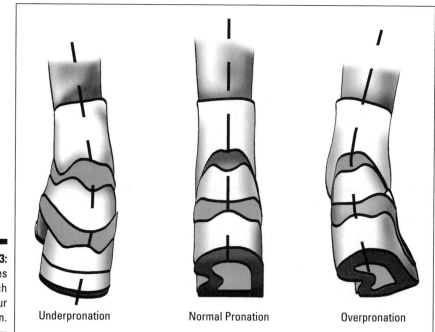

Figure 5-3:
Buy shoes
that match
your
pronation.

Underpronation   Normal Pronation   Overpronation

Fit to Be Tied

Biomechanical considerations not withstanding, fit is the most important aspect of choosing a shoe. If a shoe seems a tiny bit on the big side, you can get away with it by wearing a slightly thicker sock, for example, or by pulling the laces a bit tighter. You may even find to your surprise that they're just right. However, if you have even the slightest inkling that a shoe's a bit too small, don't take it. A shoe that's too tight can only result in blisters, discolored toenails, and general discomfort.

Here's a checklist to determine whether the shoe fits:

- You should be able to wiggle your toes in the *toe box,* or tip of the shoe.

- Your foot should feel snug in the heel, and there should be no "slipping" sensation. Your heel or Achilles tendon should not feel pinched to any degree either.

- You should have reasonable flexibility in the forefoot/toe area. (Try bending the shoe slightly with your hand.)

- The shoe should fit snugly across the top of the foot, but it shouldn't have a straitjacket feel, either. In addition, the tongue of the shoe should be padded enough to prevent the shoe laces from irritating, or cutting into, the top of your foot.

- If the shoes feel stiff, clunky, or generally uncomfortable during your test run, don't rationalize that they need to be broken in. Running shoe technology has advanced rapidly in the last two decades: These are not Zatopek's army boots!

How Long Should Your Shoes Last?

After you've laced on your new pair of running shoes, how long can you expect them to last? That depends. If you are a 280-pound former NFL lineman and you pound around on concrete sidewalks, your shoes won't last as long as those worn by the former 110-pound cheerleader who touches down lightly as she runs along a path of pine needles. Height, weight, running form, and the surface you run on all determine the life of your running shoe.

But generally speaking, you can expect to get between 300 and 600 miles on a quality pair of running shoes. But remember, shoes (expensive as they can be) are cheaper than paying for injury diagnosis and rehabilitation at the sports medicine clinic. So don't try to eke out 1,000 miles on a pair of shoes.

Even if the wear and tear to the upper part of a shoe that's seen 600 miles seems minimal, the shock-absorbing qualities of the shoe are most likely long gone. Relegate those old shoes to chores such as lawn-cutting or dog-walking, but don't be tempted to run a few more workouts in them once you suspect they're shot.

"Running on worn-out shoes is like driving on bald tires," says one running shop owner. "You might make the next town, but then again, you might have a blow out."

As in relationships, you get big points in the shoe game for loyalty! That means, once you have a good thing, don't go flirting around for something you *think* may be better just because it looks sleek and sexy and has good hype. If you find a shoe that works well for you (that is, you've run in the same make and model for two years and never had an injury), don't just switch for the sake of switching!

Does "Light" Make Right?

Although you may physically be able to run faster in a light shoe, leave the slipperlike, light-as-a-feather racing shoes to advanced runners. Some racing shoes weigh as little as 6 to 9 ounces, but often these models have been stripped of shock absorbing and motion control features (all which add to the weight of the shoe) in deference to pure speed.

On the other hand, you shouldn't run your local 5-K in a "clunker" (a very heavy model) that could support your local sumo wrestler. You do have some options. Ask your local running store people about "lightweight" trainers, a shoe that weighs a bit less than everyday training shoes but has more motion control and shock absorption qualities than a pure racing shoe. Some runners alternate wearing their heavy training shoes (13 to 15 ounces in weight) with a lighter version (usually around 10 ounces in weight) that they lace up for quality sessions or the occasional race or fun run.

Never run (speaking in terms of miles, here) in your tennis or basketball shoes, and certainly don't play court sports in your running shoes. Running shoes lack the support for side-to-side movement, increasing your chances of a turned ankle.

FLO-JO SAYS

If the shoe fits . . .

Over the years, I've worn lots of shoes from different manufacturers. While the shoes were of high quality, they lacked the flair and style that's very much a part of my personality. So, years ago, I decided that I would design a shoe that was not only comfortable and durable for performance, but that also looked good.

I've been fortunate to partner with Saucony to develop and manufacture a line of shoes and apparel — with the specific needs of women in mind. Designing this new product line allowed me to share with women my sense of style and fashion.

Other Stuff to Maybe Buy Besides Shoes

You don't *really* need a lot of the gadgets that are marketed for runners. What you need, truthfully, is a good pair of shoes and whatever you consider to be comfortable clothing. But some items certainly can enhance your running, either by providing more feedback for training, more comfort, or even protection from possible dangers.

A word about clothes

You've probably seen very serious-looking runners wearing tight Lycra pants or shorts and a shirt made out of some space-age material. You've also probably seen runners wearing sweats from top to bottom (no matter what the weather is like) à la Sylvester Stallone in the *Rocky* movies. If you're a beginner, we have very simple advice for you:

✔ Wear light, comfortable clothes that are appropriate for the weather.

✔ Avoid pants or shorts that chafe.

That's really about it. You shouldn't worry that much about what you're wearing. You're better off devoting energy to getting comfortable with your running routine and sticking to it.

Watch your time

You can purchase a plastic running watch for less than a dinner at a good restaurant. For about $30, you can get the most basic watch. But if you want waterproof, glow-in-the-dark, alarm-clock, multibeep models, you're getting into the $100-plus range. Although you don't absolutely need a running watch, it's a nice thing to have to time the duration of your workouts and to monitor your pulse rate.

Keep the beat

Heart monitors can be of major importance for the following reasons:

- ✔ Your doctor thinks that you need to monitor your levels of exertion for medical reasons.
- ✔ You're an advanced athlete looking to train at specific rates and gearing toward high performance.
- ✔ You are a habitual overtrainer who can benefit from a device that helps hold you back.

Otherwise, don't be in a big hurry to purchase a heart monitor if you are just starting a running program. You can always consider getting one if you become a lifetime runner with an eye toward improving performance in competition.

If you do decide to shop for heart monitors, consider the Polar brand. They have a good variety of models to choose from and has historically been a leader in the industry.

Made with the shades

Amazingly enough, some high-end, high-tech sunglasses can cost as much — or more — than a pair of running shoes. (And running shoes do better if you forget and leave them on the car seat.) Although you don't need top-of-the-line shades, strongly consider a pair that features 100-percent protection from ultraviolet (UV) rays. Good sports shades can also be a general comfort-boosting accessory. Squinting your way through the last 2 miles of a morning or late afternoon run straight into a fiery red sun isn't a lot of fun. Even winter running can expose you to lots of reflective glare off fields of snow. Shades, plus sun block and a hat with a brim, can cut down on intrusive rays, no matter what the season. Sport sunglasses can also protect you from dust, insects bent on a crash course, and other airborne particles.

Chapter 6
Nutrition for Runners

- -

In This Chapter

▶ The importance of water

▶ A discussion of sports drinks and alcohol

▶ Food, food, food

▶ Advice for vegetarians

▶ Advice for runners trying to lose weight

- -

During the first running boom in the early 1970s, Dr. Ernest van Aaken, a German physician/running coach, championed the cause of fitness running for all (including women) in Europe.

Van Aaken saw the negative results of the abundance of luxury in the Western industrialized nations. He noted how the convenience of cars (and other machines) and poor dietary habits had conspired to make the general population physically unfit. Although the average individual was losing both fitness and health for many reasons, the solution, van Aaken believed, was quite simple.

Van Aaken said, "My whole teaching in one sentence is: 'Run slowly, run daily, drink moderately, and don't eat like a pig.'"

That's good advice. But runners, even some who train diligently for racing, sometimes sabotage their fitness programs with a poor diet.

A recent survey shows that the average American watches four hours of television a day. But as little as 15 or 20 minutes of running, four times per week, can promote physical fitness when combined with good eating habits.

Bottoms Up

When van Aaken preached "drink moderately," he was talking about going slow on those huge steins of German beer at the Oktoberfest.

But when it comes to the body's most important nutrient — water — most runners don't drink enough. The human body is more than 70 percent water, and it soon ceases to function if its water is not replenished. (The body can function a lot longer without food than it can without water.)

Although fluid demands become obvious during a hard run on a hot afternoon (runners can lose more than 2 quarts of water in an hour), runners will do well if they hydrate throughout the day, every day. A good place to start is to drink 8 to 12 ounces of water at least six to eight times during an average day, and more when exercise or weather conditions demand it.

Keep in mind that your water needs may be even greater if you drink several cups of coffee or tea or consume alcohol on a regular basis. Caffeine and alcohol act as diuretics and increase water loss from the body with frequent urination.

During the workday, don't just buzz by the water fountain for a quick sip. Instead, fill up a bottle or paper cup and drink it all back at your desk. And head back for refills as the hours pass.

Thirst trap

Don't trust your thirst to tell you when to start drinking — or stop drinking for that matter. By the time you feel thirsty, you are already dehydrated, so drink before you feel parched. Conversely, your body will tend to shut off the thirsty message after you begin drinking, but finish off that half glass of H_2O. You need it!

Signs of dehydration can include

- A headache. Sometimes you pop an aspirin for a headache, but the water that you drink it down with may be the solution.
- Urine that's amber or yellow in color. Clear, or a very light yellow, is what you want.
- Dizziness, weakness, chills, cramps, or nausea.

Energy aid (sports) drinks

In terms of running performance, most energy aid drinks (sometimes called "sports drinks" or "fluid replacement drinks") do have something extra to offer, as opposed to just plain water. Here's what's in those drinks:

- ✔ **Carbohydrates:** An 8-ounce fluid-replacement solution is between 15 and 20 percent carbohydrates.

- ✔ **Salts (or Sodium):** You do loose salt through sweating, but the average diet (particularly if you use a sports drink) more than replenishes what your body needs.

- ✔ **Electrolytes:** Trace amounts of electrolytes (sodium) help speed fluid absorption.

- ✔ **Sugar:** Some of the sugars in the aid drinks can give a tired runner a much-needed blood sugar boost late in a race or workout.

Some runners prefer plain water as a good thirst quencher, but they also would like to benefit from the carbohydrate content of fluid-replacement aid drinks. Here's a possible solution for your next long race: Drink water at one aid station and an energy aid drink at the next, and then continue to alternate between the two throughout the race. However, since muscles typically hold enough glycogen to handle two hours of exercise, most runners can get by on just water for relatively short stints of exercise.

Brew crew

In the 1970s, more than a few road races had a post-race keg of beer (or two) sweating on ice, waiting for thirsty runners ready for a celebration. Many runners of that era would hoist a brew, wipe the foam from their lips, and proclaim, "I'm carbo loading!"

Beer, in fact, is a poor source of carbohydrates, despite the beliefs of those runners who embraced the suds a few decades back. Keep in mind that it takes less alcohol to "bring on the buzz" if you are a dehydrated, tired runner. (That's not a recommendation; it's a caution!)

Beer does offer some trace elements of copper (as does, can you believe this, chocolate!). Brewer's yeast, part of the beer-making process, also is a good source of chromium, a mineral that assists in breaking down carbohydrates for fuel. Copper is an immune system booster and also helps fight high cholesterol.

Does that mean you should dine on bars of deluxe chocolate and wash them down with microbrews, proclaiming, "I'm copper loading!"? Not with a straight face. Lean meats, clams and mussels, fish, nuts, and most vegetables and fruits can provide lots of copper.

But are beer and chocolate in moderation okay for the fitness runner? The choice is yours, of course, but a little won't hurt you. (As Shakespeare once wrote, "Dost thou think because thou are virtuous there shall be no more cakes and ale?")

Fruit of the vine

Wine, especially red wine, has gotten a lot of good press in recent years — and we're not just talking wine press here! Some studies show evidence that red wine elevates HDL cholesterol (that's the good kind) and lowers LDL cholesterol (the bad stuff). The red wine sweeps out the LDL cholesterol that tends to stick to the artery walls.

You can obtain the positive benefits of alcohol with just a few ounces. Once you go beyond one or two drinks, then you are certainly consuming alcohol for reasons other than health benefits. In fact, you're probably doing something that's not healthy at all. The bottom line is that alcohol (be it in the form of wine, beer, or "hard stuff" like vodka or whiskey) is a drug that has addictive properties for some people.

A last word on alcohol

If you are running partly to lose weight, then alcohol is a very poor beverage choice. It can make you feel tired. It's loaded with calories. And even if your running helps keep alcohol-induced weight gain at bay, booze can still have a bad effect on vital body organs. As Percy Cerutty, a famous Australian coach of Olympic champions, once said, "No amount of running can prevent the liver from cirrhosis."

If you do hoist a few beers in a post-race celebration, keep it to one or two. To prevent dehydration, make sure that you drink water first and then drink two glasses of water for each beer, in addition to eating food. If you drink more than one or two beers, hand your car keys to the person sipping mineral water. Then again, you can always "just say no!"

Eating on the Run

You can only take in a limited amount of fluid and fuel during a race. Even when you do an almost perfect job of fluid and fuel intake during a race, it's still hard to provide your body with water or carbohydrates as fast as they're expended.

If you want to do well in races, the dinner the night before the race and the breakfast on the morning of the race are important meals. Here are some menu suggestions:

- ✔ **Dinner:** Pasta and rice dishes are favorites with runners, and with good reason. Both are loaded with carbohydrates to fuel your muscles. If you eat meat, take only a small portion.

    If you opt for the runner's traditional choice of pasta, don't make the mistake of pouring on a high-fat cream sauce or cheese sauce. Instead, opt for a light red sauce that will be easier to digest.

- ✔ **Breakfast:** Your answers to two big questions here determine what you should eat. One is, how far is the race? If it's a 5-K, then half a bagel and a banana a couple hours before the race may be enough. But if you're running a half-marathon or marathon, then you're going to be out there a long time. Think pancakes, cold cereals, or oatmeal. Consider a banana, aid drink, or an energy bar or gel closer to race time.

Always test out your pre-race dinner and breakfast menus on a training run in the weeks prior to the race. That way you'll have less chance of an unpleasant surprise, such as stomach cramps and unplanned detours from the race route in search of a bathroom.

Energy gels and bars

Energy gels or bars are proven on-the-run energy boosters for runners, especially those running half-marathons and marathons. Energy gels come in tiny packets that are easy to carry in a race (especially if you tuck a couple in a pair of racing gloves) and typically provide between 70 and 100 calories. A water "chaser" helps gels and bars go down easier.

Bars and gels come in many different flavors (banana, peanut butter crunch, chocolate, and so on) these days, so you can suit your taste buds at the same time you give your body an energy boost.

Approach energy gels, bars, and sports drinks with caution

Despite what the advertising for energy gels, bars and sports drinks may lead you to believe, you can still run and run well without them. Indeed, some nutritionists advise against regular use of these products, primarily because of their high sugar (and, in some cases, fat and calorie) content.

During heavy training or long-distance events, these products can be a real boost. For example, research has shown, fairly conclusively, that in endurance events of 90 minutes or more, a sports or carbohydrate drink can enhance performance. But don't assume that you need to wolf down two energy bars before a 3-mile run or drink a quart of sports drink daily. Use these products, but use them wisely — and don't make them part of your regular diet. Day in and day out, you can make better food choices to keep you on the go. Gels, bars, and sports drinks should be regarded as compliments — not replacements — in your day-to-day diet.

Some races, especially long endurance events such as triathlons or ultra-marathons, offer bananas or orange slices at their aid stations. Bananas are a top-notch pick for endurance athletes: A medium-sized piece of the yellow fruit checks in with around 100 to 110 calories and is high on carbohydrates (around 90 percent of the calories are carbos) and very low on fat.

Before you try energy bars or gels or aid drinks in a race situation, experiment with them — several times — in hard workouts. That way you'll discover what works best with your stomach and meets your energy needs.

Carbos

Some runners pick the right foods to eat the day before and morning of a race and are diligent about taking in fluids during the competition. But many of those same runners don't eat so "smart" in those weeks between races.

Dietary habits can affect performance and, more importantly, overall health. A solid place to start is with the carbohydrates rule! Since runners constantly must "keep the furnace stoked" (you burn about 100 calories per mile run), shoot for a diet that is about 60 percent carbohydrates.

Marathoners have a good reason for devouring big bowls of pasta and chunks of bread the night before they tackle 26.2 miles of running: Carbohydrates, or carbos as endurance athletes like to call them, are the body's primary source of energy. A typical runner's engine runs hot enough to burn fats and protein, as well, but the working body prefers to stoke with carbos.

Nutritionists divide carbohydrates into two camps — simple carbohydrates and complex carbohydrates. Simple carbohydrates are found in soft drinks, candy bars, and pastries. As a rule, simple carbohydrates aren't the best source of energy because they often bring along a high percentage of fat, like what you find in a dozen donuts, for example. Simple carbohydrates can also contain a lot of sugar. If a food has large amounts of fat and sugar calories, then that particular source is unlikely to hold any significant amount of vitamins, minerals, or fiber. Nutritionists say that these kinds of foods hold "empty calories."

However, some foods with high sugar content do have plenty to offer in the way of minerals or vitamins. Certain fruits — such as bananas, oranges, apples, and raisins — break down into fructose (a natural fruit sugar) but are good carbohydrate sources. These kinds of fruits are better snack choices than fat-laden foods such as candy bars.

Some athletes believe that honey — because it's more natural — has more nutritional merit than refined white sugar. But honey, maple syrup, and sugar (brown or white) are all equally lacking in terms of vitamins or minerals. Brown sugar, however, does have a small amount of calcium.

Good sources of complex carbohydrates include grains, breads, vegetables, and beans. These foods take longer to convert to glucose (sugars) and are then stored as glycogen (stored dietary sugars) in the muscles or liver, to be used for energy when called upon during physical activity.

Runners typically eat a lot of carbohydrates, but it's still easy to run low on the body's best fuel source. As we mentioned, runners burn up around 100 calories per mile. If you are training for a 10-K, half-marathon, or marathon and running even 30 to 40 miles per week in preparation, then you are burning a lot of calories.

A "trained" muscle can store more glycogen than an "untrained" muscle — in some cases, 50 percent more. So if you run consistently, your muscles will learn to store more energy. The more glycogen the muscles can store, the longer they can perform.

To keep up with the calories burned, a runner who weighs 150 pounds needs to take in somewhere between 2,500 and 5,000 calories per day. Keeping in mind that a runner burns about 100 calories per mile, obviously a profes-sional marathoner training 100 miles per week has bigger needs than the fitness runner logging 30 miles per week. But the trick is to limit (but not eliminate) the number of fat calories in your daily diet.

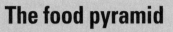

The food pyramid

Man — even a running man — cannot exist on carbohydrates alone. The same goes for women. Although carbohydrates make up the solid base of the USDA's Food Guide Pyramid (see the following figure), proteins and even some fat figure in a well-balanced diet.

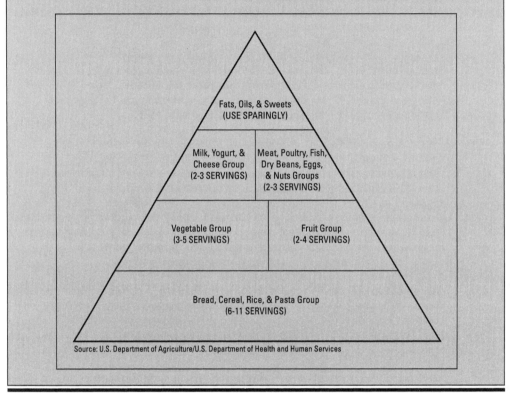

Fats, Oils, & Sweets
(USE SPARINGLY)

Milk, Yogurt, &
Cheese Group
(2-3 SERVINGS)

Meat, Poultry, Fish,
Dry Beans, Eggs,
& Nuts Groups
(2-3 SERVINGS)

Vegetable Group
(3-5 SERVINGS)

Fruit Group
(2-4 SERVINGS)

Bread, Cereal, Rice, & Pasta Group
(6-11 SERVINGS)

Source: U.S. Department of Agriculture/U.S. Department of Health and Human Services

A heavy lunch that provides 1,000 calories or more can cause you to feel drowsy or sluggish in the late afternoon. Opt for light mid-day choices, such as fruit and yogurt, to stay energized and alert. If you are looking for something more, consider a bowl of your favorite soup and half a sandwich.

Protein power

Some runners treat protein as an afterthought. They figure it's more for weight lifters tossing the big plates around at the health club, or for NFL linemen battering the sled in practice.

However, runners need protein as well. Yes, protein is the body's third choice (behind carbohydrates and fats) when it comes to body fuel. But protein is king in certain areas because of its ability to build or repair muscle tissue with amino acids.

Iron men (and women)

Iron is one of the most important minerals for an endurance athlete. That's because it's an essential part of hemoglobin, the protein that transports oxygen from the lungs to the muscles during exercise. Runners suffering from iron deficiency — called anemia — will tire much sooner than those who follow an iron-rich diet.

People who are at high risk for not getting enough iron include the following:

- ✔ Runners who eat no, or very little, red meat, including some strict vegetarians
- ✔ Female runners who lose iron during their menstrual cycle
- ✔ Runners who lose iron through heavy sweating

Here are some ways to boost your iron intake. Cook in a cast-iron skillet. Include a vitamin C-rich food with each meal. For example, drink a glass of orange juice or squirt lemon juice on fish or chicken dishes. Occasionally make lean, red meats part of your diet.

Think zinc

Just as with iron, meat is the best source of readily available zinc. Zinc is an important mineral for runners because it's a top defender of the immune system.

If you are a chronic cold-catcher, you may be low on zinc, or you may be over-training, or both. One of the best sources of zinc is oysters (also rumored to improve your love life, but that's another story!), followed by red meat and other shellfish sources, such as crab.

Calcium club

Do you need a milk mustache to get enough of bone-building calcium? Not absolutely, but dairy products are a great source of calcium. Calcium is essential for runners because it helps guard against stress fractures, a bone injury that can knock you out of training for six weeks or more.

Good sources of calcium include

✔ Lowfat milk and lowfat yogurt

✔ Broccoli, kale, and spinach

✔ Canned salmon

Fight the fat (but keep some, too!)

Repeat after us: Fat is not all bad! In fact, some fats — such as the omega fatty acids found in fish, certain nuts, and vegetable oils — can help you stay healthy. (Research shows omega fats can bolster your immune system.) Very lowfat diets, in fact, can put you in a moody funk, according to some studies.

No, you can't expect life-long health if you gorge yourself on cheeseburgers and fat-fried onion rings seven days a week, but your body does need some fat. The trick is to avoid most animal fats and the saturated fats found in some of those highly processed snack foods.

Then there are some fatty treats that, if used in moderation, can offer some vitamins. Ice cream is a reasonable good source of calcium, but runners — especially those combining exercise and diet to lose weight — should indulge in it sparingly. That's because it contains a lot of saturated fat; some of the primo brands (yeah, they taste yummy!) get half their calories from fat.

Good fat, bad fat

At least one-quarter of your total blood cholesterol should be the "good guy" — high density lipoprotein, or HDL. HDL is like the cavalry to the rescue that sweeps out the LDL (low density lipoprotein), which is the waxlike "bad guy" that wants to gum up your arteries and decrease blood flow to your heart.

Here's yet another good reason to lace on your shoes and log some miles: When you log those miles, you unclog your arteries. Endurance athletes (runners, cyclists, and swimmers) lead the pack when it comes to elevated HDL.

Avoid sabotage

One of the sneaky ways that fat slips into your diet is in the "extra" category. For example, a sizzling hamburger is already high in fat. (The fast-food kind can approach a whopping 40 percent!) Then if you add two slices of cheese and smoother it all with mayonnaise, you're loading fat on top of fat. Instead, opt for an onion slice and a bit of green lettuce on top of the burger.

The American Heart Association sets 30 percent as an acceptable fat level in your daily diet, but if you have high cholesterol, your doctor may urge you to shoot for under 20 percent.

Here are some other fat-fighting strategies:

- ✔ Feel your oats — or at least, eat 'em! Foods such as oatmeal and oat bran are rich in cholesterol-lowering fiber.

- ✔ Go for 2 percent milk instead of whole milk. You'll get lots of calcium and protein but less fat. Skim milk is even better for fat-fighting.

- ✔ Try something fishy. Salmon, tuna, and halibut — among other fishes — are great sources of omega-3 fatty acids. Omega-3 fatty acids are high on the good-guy list and help fight heart disease.

Should you ban all fats from your diet? First of all, that would virtually be impossible. Second, your body does need some fat (to keep warm, for example) and will burn fat (especially on long slow workouts), although it prefers to stoke carbohydrates.

I was raised on butter and lots of it! When I grew older and began serious training, I tried to cut butter out of my diet altogether, but I craved it all the time. I think that when it comes to food that you really crave, the best thing to do is allow yourself to indulge just a little every once in a while. Total abstinence doesn't always work, so if you manage the times when you indulge, you can avoid the guilt.

Help for Vegetarians

Is it impossible for vegetarians to get enough protein, iron, and zinc? No, but it does take some extra effort and research.

For example, a 150-pound runner needs about 90 grams of protein per day to replenish damaged muscle proteins after a hard workout. One small beefsteak or 12 ounces of tuna would do the trick. But vegetarians would need five cups of cooked lentils (a good source of non-meat protein) to approach the 90 grams of needed protein.

If red meat isn't likely to end up on your menu but chicken is acceptable, then add a few bits of chicken to your next bowl of lentil soup. The absorption rate of available iron will more than double.

Runners on a non-meat diet need to do a bit of sleuthing to find all the zinc they can from other sources. Black-eyed peas, garbanzo beans, lentils, brown rice, wheat germ, and almonds should be high on the vegetarian runner's shopping list.

Runners who are strict vegetarians (those who won't eat foods produced by animals, such as cheese or eggs) need to zero in on what little iron sources they can grab from plant foods. In truth, most plants either are poor sources of iron or don't easily surrender their iron sources. Spinach is a good example of the latter type of plant.

Some decent non-meat sources for iron (in addition to lentils) include

- Dried fruits, such as apricots or prunes
- Fortified breakfast cereals (especially if you add raisins or dates)
- Fortified juices, such as orange juice
- Beans (kidney, mung, and baked varieties, and bean curd cakes)
- Blackstrap molasses, brewer's yeast, and wheat germ
- Daily multi-vitamin with iron

Fighting the Good Fight

Keep on top of dietary tips that can improve your performance and overall health. Here are a few ways to improve your nutrition:

- Add some color. Fruits and vegetables that are yellow or orange in color tend to be good sources of cancer-fighting beta-carotene.
- Fast food almost always means fat food. Pay special attention when you travel and are forced to eat in a hurry.
- Cut down on your coffee habit gradually by adding milk over several weeks. Drink it light! You can get some extra calcium in your diet, and slowly cut down on the java.
- Just a modest serving of strawberries can supply more than half your daily vitamin C needs. Ditto for green peppers.
- Tomato sauce may reduce a man's risk of prostate cancer. Alfredo sauce made with heavy cream has been called a "heart attack on a plate" by one nutritionist. So what do you want on *your* pasta?

✔ Fruits such as oranges and bananas are good potassium sources. Potassium helps a runner's muscles contract and can fight muscle cramps.

✔ Trade in the trendy high-fat ice cream for a lowfat yogurt. You'll save a bundle of fat calories and get more energy.

✔ Try nonfat yogurt as a substitute for sour cream on a baked spud or in recipes.

✔ Broil or bake chicken (instead of frying it) and remove the skin to cut down on fat.

✔ When you have a choice between eggs (especially Eggs Benedict) or cereal, go for the grain! Then slice some bananas or strawberries on top.

✔ Pretzels are high in carbohydrates and low in fat. They are a super snack choice (along with figs or raisins) when stacked up against fat-heavy chips, most snack crackers, or fries.

✔ Read labels! Be alert for fat percentages and high sodium and sugar levels.

✔ Get crunchy. Raw veggies (like red pepper or carrot sticks) make good lowfat snacks and are high in vitamins A and C.

✔ Pancakes are a great carbohydrate source (about 75 percent carbohydrates, in fact). With maple syrup and just a modest amount of butter, you can still keep the fat content under 20 percent.

✔ Don't forget to reload! Your muscles are most receptive to replenishing glycogen within the first hour after you finish a hard run or workout.

✔ With all the concern about eating too many calories, keep in mind that not enough will leave you without energy, too. Learn the signs of eating disorders and seek help if you (or those around you, such as teammates, coaches, or family members) suspect you are headed for trouble.

Running, Diet, and Weight Loss

The Zone Diet. The Atkins Diet. The Beverly Hills Diet. The "This" Diet. The "That" Diet. Remember one important fact about diets: They don't work if there's no exercise to go along with them. In fact, studies have shown that most people who lose weight on some of these fad diets eventually gain it back if they don't exercise.

And if you want an exercise that really burns calories and is also convenient and efficient, there's no exercise like running.

If you're trying to shed a few pounds, follow these tips, compiled from a number of nutritionists and weight loss experts. They can help tilt the scale in your favor:

- Instead of looking for some magic food or weight loss concoction, eat balanced meals and keep portion sizes smaller. Stick with the USDA Food Pyramid, which makes vegetables, fruits, and whole grains the foundation of a healthy diet. Or use the American Heart Association Step I diet, which recommends that 55 to 60 percent of your calories come from carbohydrates, 15 to 10 percent from protein, and 25 to 30 percent from fat.

- Set a goal. For some, it may be an upcoming wedding. For others, the incentive might be a reunion, vacation, or milestone birthday. Whatever the goal, if it motivates you to finally take action, great. But remember that you've got to make a life-long commitment to this lifestyle change — a change that includes proper eating, as well as running. Don't aim for, say, your brother's wedding, and then let yourself backslide as soon as the vows are exchanged and the photos are taken.

- Lose weight sensibly. A safe, reasonable goal for weight loss is 1 pound a week. That may not sound like much, but if you add it up over a year, that's over 50 pounds!

- The tale of the scale can be a misleading one because so many factors can influence daily weight fluctuations. So don't make yourself a slave to the weigh-in. Instead, weigh yourself no more than once a week, and at the same time of day, so that you have a meaningful basis of comparison.

- To lose weight, lift weight. The more lean muscle mass you have, the more calories you'll burn. Running alone will not do this. You need to do some form of resistance or weight training, which we discuss in Chapter 17.

- Finally, get moving. Although being overweight is not good, research now suggests that being sedentary may be even worse. Running can be your key to weight loss.

Part II
Basic Training

The 5th Wave   By Rich Tennant

Apparently what happens is, they try to push a tree over. When they find out they can't, they go running off in frustration.

In this part . . .

This part focuses on improving your training program after you've made the commitment to begin running. We show what constitutes good form; we help you to warm up, stretch, and cool down; we describe the benefits of hill training; and we provide advice on running safely in all kinds of situations.

Chapter 7
Elements of Style

. . . .

In This Chapter

▶ Finding a comfortable form

▶ Moving your arms correctly

▶ Striding correctly

. . . .

*B*ill Bowerman, the legendary Oregon mentor and coach of the 1972 U.S. Olympic Track and Field team, once quipped: "God determines how fast you are. I can only help with the mechanics."

Along similar lines of thought, someone once asked a top-notch Swedish physiologist what was the most crucial element in the making of an Olympic champion. "Choosing good parents," stated the sports scientist.

But even if you weren't blessed with Olympic genetics and heavenly talents, you can improve your own times — and feel more comfortable even while running at faster speeds — simply by consistent training. Many recreational runners, especially novices, overlook the fact that running form is a piece of the training puzzle.

Running is easy because it simply requires putting one foot in front of the other . . . right? Well, not exactly. To get the most benefit from running, you need to develop a form that is comfortable and efficient for you. Running forms can range from the barely functional plod that resembles a forced march to the poetry-in-motion style of Olympic champions. When it comes to a natural running style, most runners fall somewhere in between, but almost all of us can benefit from a little advice to help improve our form.

Cruise in Comfort

Good running form can improve your levels of running comfort, especially for the beginning runner. Improving your form also can help you run faster, but that's more of a concern among experienced runners.

Good form: Give it time

Remember that it takes time to develop good form. When I started running and competing at the age of 7, I had the worst form of anyone else running, and my coaches told me that if I wanted to improve my times, I had to improve my running form. I used to just show up at races and run, and no one actually taught me how to change my running form until I was in college.

After running for all those years with poor mechanics, it me took several more years to change. I worked very hard every day at practice, making sure I concentrated on running with good mechanics. What used to be just a simple break-neck run when I was a little girl turned into some pretty technical training that involved a great deal of mental effort.

Even if you're not training for the Olympics, good form just feels better. Trust me. Running should be fun, but if you concentrate on your form and work at it while you train, eventually, good form will come to you almost naturally, and you'll run better times and feel more comfortable doing so.

How do you know whether your form might need work? If you grunt, grimace, grind, and pound your way through a run and then you limp home 15 minutes later, you may want to consider changing your style. Running should not be a sport that makes you wonder whether the second running boom should instead be called the "running doom."

However, if you learn to "float" — regardless of your body type or your capacity for speed — with smooth, rhythmic strides and arm action, then running becomes a graceful pleasure that enables you to comfortably tour your surrounding world.

Gritting your teeth and clenching your fists tightly in an all-out effort is good running only if that running involves a 1-yard plunge across the goal line in the NFL. Long-distance running, by contrast, requires relaxation.

Style Points

Where do you start when you're working on your style? At the top, of course. Here are some pointers about upper-body style:

✔ Keep your head straight, with your chin level or slightly tucked. Your head should not be flung back, as if madly dashing for the commuter train. Look straight ahead or look out and just slightly down. Don't look directly down at your feet unless you are negotiating potential ankle-turning terrain.

✔ Shoulders should be squared (not rounding in), and your chest should be thrust (slightly) up and out. This form allows more oxygen into your lungs. Keep your back straight. Don't hunch! A sagging running style or bending forward will inhibit oxygen intake.

✔ Although your back should be straight ("Run tall!" coaches often implore their charges), don't be as ramrod rigid as a West Point plebe. Avoid thrusting your shoulders back so hard that you seem to be forcing the shoulder blades together; doing so can result in tight neck, back, and shoulder muscles.

✔ Your jaw should be relaxed and slack. Your mouth should be open for optimal breathing. Don't squint or wince. (On sunny days, sports shades will help a lot.) Relax your face muscles!

Figure 7-1 illustrates proper upper-body style.

Figure 7-1: Keep your head level, shoulders square, and your back straight.

Arm Yourself for High-Powered Running

Good running involves more than just the legs, heart, and lungs. Proper arm carriage and arm action play a big supporting role in achieving a smooth, efficient style. Arm action plays a part in both your stride frequency and stride length.

Stride frequency is the number of strides that a runner takes over a certain time period — regardless whether that duration is 20 seconds, 1 minute, or 1 hour. Stride frequency and stride length are the two major determining speed factors for runners.

Here's a checklist for proper arm form:

- ✔ Keep an approximate 90-degree angle in the elbow. Try not to break the angle in your elbow as you swing your arms back.

- ✔ Carry your arms at waist level or slightly above waist level. As your arm swings up, it should come up to about your collarbone. As your fore-arm comes down, it will initiate your backswing.

- ✔ Pretend that a line is drawn down the center of your chest. Avoid crossing your arms over the imaginary center line during the phases of your arm swing. Cross-over arms can result in a twisting motion — from the hips and waist — that sabotages running efficiency.

- ✔ Cup your hands, with the thumb resting lightly on top of the hand, thumb nail facing up. You should not clench your hands in a tight fist, but neither should you run with open palms or a "doggy paddle" motion.

- ✔ On the backswing, the fingers of your cupped hand should lightly brush the side of your running shorts. The complete motion of the hand should look as if you are reaching for your wallet in a back pocket and then swinging forward again as if you are ready to shake hands.

Pretend that you are running with a powder-blue robin's egg in each cupped hand. Hold your hands closed with such a light degree of pressure that assures that you won't crush or drop the tiny imaginary eggs as you complete your run.

Tightening the hands can cause other muscles in your arms to tighten, which can restrict your natural movement. So keep your hands relaxed while running.

Hitting Your Stride

When it comes to foot strike, most runners naturally land on the heel and then "roll up" to push off with the ball of the foot or toes. Midfoot strikers push off with the ball of the foot, and those rare forefoot strikers push off with their toes.

Ideally, runners should land lightly on the heel, with the lead leg just slightly bent at the knee (the best method to absorb shock), immediately roll up to the forefoot or toes, and push off powerfully into the next stride.

Here's a form checklist for the legs:

- ✔ Land lightly on the heel or midfoot, preferably with your lead leg bent slightly at the knee to help absorb shock. Avoid "reaching" with your lead leg.

- ✔ Knee lift should be minimal (except on very steep hills) because too much up-and-down movement results in wasted energy.

- ✔ When the leg swings back, you should feel a "flicking" sensation with the heel and ankle. But the flick should not be so much that you are close to kicking yourself in the buttocks.

- ✔ Run in a straight line. Make sure that your feet land in parallel paths and do not cross over. Crossover foot strikes are a sure sign of too much twisting and wasted motion.

- ✔ After each foot strike, drive into your next stride with a good push off the toes or forefoot.

Pitfalls of footfalls

Novices are often tempted to lengthen their stride in an attempt to cover more ground. Although increasing your stride length is one way to run faster, it more often than not results in overstriding. Overstriding, in fact, slows a runner down because it increases impact (and, because of that, injury risk) and takes you longer to get back to your center of gravity and begin the next stride.

You are overstriding if you habitually "reach" with your lead leg in a virtually straight position. When your leg is straight, the first contact with the ground occurs hard on the heel. The end result is a lot of shock shimmering up through the lower leg and shins, possibly affecting even your hips and back.

So what's the trick? The way to effectively increase stride length — without falling into the trap of overstriding — is to improve overall flexibility and muscle strength. It's not a quick fix and requires a modest (but consistent) stretching program and some strength-enhancing running sessions, such as a weekly hill session.

A good weight training program, one that addresses the needs of runners, can improve overall muscle strength, too. But some renowned coaches, most notably Arthur Lydiard of New Zealand (often called the father of modern distance running methods), believe that hill workouts (see Chapter 9) are the best way to build muscle strength that runners need.

The goal to increase natural stride length without overstriding requires

- ✔ Creating muscles that have a greater range of motion, in effect, increased flexibility.
- ✔ Developing stronger muscles capable of pushing off with greater power.

The end result should be a slight increase in stride length that is still within your natural gait. (Overstriding is the enemy of progress!) The gain may be so gradual and small that the average runner may have difficulty noticing. The increased stride length is simply a fringe benefit of your increased flexibility and muscle strength.

Rev up your stride rate

For beginning runners, increasing stride frequency is easier to achieve than increasing stride length. Some of the increased stride rate will just come naturally as you get in shape, but you can make major gains by performing high-quality workouts, including even modest speed sessions on the track. Some specific drills, incorporated into your warm-up several times a week, can lay a foundation for an increase in your stride rate.

Some coaches refer to stride frequency or stride rate as *leg turnover*. The average recreational runner takes about 80 to 85 strides per minute, but most Olympic-class runners can crank out a stride rate in the mid-90s over a minute.

An easy drill to add to your running program is "striders" of about 100 yards in length — the length of your basic football field. You should run these briskly, with smooth running form, but not "all out." (For example, if it takes you 15 seconds to run the length of a football field as fast as you can, then run your strider drill closer to 20 seconds per 100 yards.) Try the strider drill two or three times a week, either before or after your easy distance run.

I practice proper mechanics for both my upper and lower body and include form drills as part of my warm-up. Knowing that my arm action can dictate my stride length and influence stride rate, I try to keep focused on my arms in particular. But sometimes on my long runs, I have to remind myself not to get lazy and to keep active with my arms.

Another good drill to improve stride frequency is called *hot coals*. Envision that you are running on a bed of hot coals and you want to "quick step" your way over them. Practice this routine for about 50 yards (perhaps 10 seconds in duration for each hot coal rep) — just long enough so that your feet don't get burned. As with striders, this drill can be part of your warm-up or cool-down.

Running up short flights of stairs, landing on each step, is another drill that can boost your stride frequency. Hit every step as quickly as you can and then walk down for rest. (Try this in small doses — no more than once or twice a week, perhaps for as little as 5 minutes' worth to start — and try alternative workouts, such as hill running, if you experience knee pain.)

If you run five or six days per week, consider taking one day as a "form day." The session shouldn't be a killer in a physical sense, but it can be a day to tune into proper running form and try some running drills.

Exception to the rule

Good running form certainly helps with comfort and performance, but there are some notable exceptions. Emil Zatopek, the great Czech runner and winner of four Olympic gold medals, had a notoriously odd running style. Zatopek flailed his arms and contorted his face to such an extent that sportswriters nicknamed him "Emil the Terrible."

But Zatopek was extremely dedicated and mentally tough. He ran harder workouts than any of his rivals in the post-World War II era, so he still won. As for his agonized expression on the track, Zatopek reminded his critics that no one received any extra points for picture-book running style: "This is not ice skating or gymnastics, you know."

However, unlike Zatopek, most of us mere mortals need all the style points we can gather to help us succeed in the running game.

Chapter 8

Warming Up, Stretching Out, and Cooling Down

In This Chapter

▶ Getting your muscles warmed up

▶ Loosening up with stretches

▶ Moving to cool down

*W*hat's the first thing you do in the morning when you get into your car? Turn the ignition and floor it? Start 'er up and let 'er rip? Of course not. You give your car's engine a few seconds — on a cold day, even a few minutes — to warm up. You need to do the same thing with your own, personal engine. Your body needs time to warm up before you hit the road.

Once upon a time, runners would bend over and touch their toes a couple times and say, "We're ready!" They were indeed ready — for any number of muscle pulls, strains, sprains, aches, and tears. A cold muscle is more susceptible to any and all such injuries. And although stretching is important, it's not the best way to get your muscles warmed up.

The Right Way to Warm Up

A warm-up is not a few haphazard stretches. If you want to warm up, try any sort of movement, such as walking, slow jogging, cycling on a stationary bike, or even just some easy calisthenics. Moving like this for at least 5 to 10 minutes is designed to gradually raise the body's core temperature, loosen up the muscles, and ease the body into a run.

Brisk walking is the ideal warm-up for running. The perfect way to get your body ready for a little more serious action is to walk a lap or two around the track or a few blocks around your neighborhood. And don't take off like an Indy 500 driver when the green flag drops when you do start walking. Begin slowly and gradually pick up the speed.

Stop: Stretching Ahead!

Although stretching itself does not a warm-up make, stretching is an important part of a running and fitness regimen, especially for runners. After putting some mileage on the personal odometer, runners' muscles tend to become tight and inflexible, especially in certain areas such as the hips, lower back, and hamstring. And when tight muscles compromise the ability of a joint's ability to move through its full range of motion, injury is more likely. Regular stretching can loosen those muscles up and improve range of motion, thereby helping to prevent injuries.

Many runners blow off stretching because it's dull, static, and slow — everything that running is not. Our response: Stretch anyway. It feels good, and you'll notice the difference during and after your run.

When to stretch?

Runners debate the issue of the best time to stretch. Some experts say that you should stretch before you run; some say after. Don't worry too much about when you stretch; just make sure that you do stretch, at some point, preferably every day. You can even stretch later in the day, while you're watching TV or before you go to bed.

How to stretch?

A stretch is a stretch, right? Well, not really. Stretching and the different ways to stretch are topics of controversy among runners.

For the past 25 years, so-called *static* or *gradual stretching* has been considered the right way to stretch. This is a slow, gradual stretch that you hold for 15 to 30 seconds. You can choose from dozens of static stretches, for almost every major muscle group; some of the stretches are almost instinctive, like the arms-reaching-for-the-sky stretch that many of us do when we first wake up in the morning.

But recently, the stretching arena has become crowded with different and new forms of flexibility training. *Ballistic stretching,* which consists of those bouncing exercises that you used to do in your junior high gym class, seems to be making a comeback. A new form of stretching called *active isolated* (AI) has gained popularity in recent years, especially among athletes. Active isolated stretching involves brief contractions of the agonist muscle to help stretch the opposite, or antagonist, muscle (the quadriceps versus the hamstrings, say), sometimes by using a rope or chord to help.

Other forms of stretching require the assistance of a trained "stretcher" (as in someone to stretch you, the "stretchee"). Stretching machines are now available on the market, too.

Some stretching techniques are new, and some are very old. Yoga, for example, is an ancient form of flexibility and relaxation exercise that has gained new converts among sore runners. Taking a yoga class is a wonderful complement to a running program. But you don't have to assume the lotus position to get the benefits of stretching. Most experts agree that you can't really go wrong with static stretching.

Stretching: The truth

Here's how to perform a stretch. Get into the proper position and hold it for 15 to 30 seconds. Don't bounce or force the motion. Go as far as you can, without feeling pain. If you feel some mild tension, that's okay, but you should not be in pain. Repeat the stretch. Remember that stretching is not a contest. Some people are naturally more flexible than others. But everybody can improve.

The flexible five

No, the "flexible five" are not some lanky, loose-jointed swing combo, but a regimen of five basic stretches that you can do if you're pressed for time. Do them every day, or at least on the days that you run.

Remember to stay relaxed while you stretch, and don't hold your breath. Breathe as you stretch.

Calf stretch

Stretching guru Bob Anderson calls the calf "the second heart of the body" because the calf is a major circulation area in the push-off phase of the running motion. To stretch out the calf, lean against a wall with your fore-arms in front of you, as shown in Figure 8-1. Position your forward leg with your toe close to the wall. Bend the knee of your forward leg and slowly move your hips forward, keeping your lower back flat and the heel of your straight leg on the ground. Hold and repeat. Then do the other leg.

Lower back, hip, groin, and hamstring stretch

This exercise is a simple and simply wonderful stretch for a runner, and you've probably done it thousands of times. Stand with your feet about shoulder width apart and pointed straight ahead. Slowly bend forward, keeping the knees "soft" (slightly bent). If you can touch your toes, fine. If you can't, fine. Feeling the stretch in your hamstrings and lower back is the key to this stretch.

Figure 8-1:
The calf
stretch.

Quadriceps stretch

You've probably seen runners do the quadriceps stretch — and most of them are doing it incorrectly. They bend their upper bodies as if they're turning themselves over like teapots, using their leg as the handle. To do this stretch correctly, take your left foot with your right hand, while using your left hand to support your body against a wall. Gently pull your heel towards your backside, keeping the rest of the body straight. Feel the stretch in the *quadriceps* (thigh) muscles. Repeat with the other side, taking your right foot with your left hand. If you have particulary well-stretched quadriceps, you're likely to be able to grab your right foot with your right hand and your left foot with your left hand when you perform this stretch — without losing your balance (see Figure 8-2).

Hamstring stretch

Because a runner's *hamstrings* (the large muscles in the back of the thigh) tend to get tight, loosen 'em up with this version of the classic old hurdler's stretch. From a seated position, extend your right leg and bend your left leg, touching the inside of your right thigh with the sole of the left foot. Grasp the part of your extended leg that you can comfortably reach, as shown in Figure 8-3. Some people can touch their foot, and others may not be able to reach much past their knee. Slowly and gently bend from the hip. Don't worry about being able to reach your toes or touch your chest to your leg. Just go as far as you can comfortably, feeling that stretch in your hamstrings. Then repeat, with left leg extended.

Figure 8-2:
Stretching a
quadricep.

Shoulders and neck stretch

Your upper body can get tense while you run, and it will definitely get tense if you do what most Americans do when not running — sit in front of a computer screen or a TV. So a little shoulder and neck stretch will help loosen you up all around. Raise the top of your shoulders towards your ears until you feel a slight tension in your neck and shoulders. Hold for 3 to 5 seconds and then relax your shoulders. Repeat several times.

Figure 8-3:
Stretching
out a
hamstring.
Don't worry
if you can't
reach your
foot or
touch your
head to
your knee.

Cool Out!

You've finished your run. What's the first thing you should do? Stop, right? Wrong. Keep moving. That's the way to prevent the blood from pooling in the legs and keep it circulating back through the heart and into the brain. (People sometimes feel dizzy if they suddenly stop moving after a hard workout.)

A post-workout cool-down after you finish running keeps the blood flowing. The blood flow, in turn, can help minimize soreness by flushing out the waste products that build up as a result of running. Five to 10 minutes of walking after a run is a cool way to cool down.

Chapter 9
Just for the Hill of It

. . . .

In This Chapter

▶ Starting out small

▶ Keeping good form uphill

▶ Going downhill

▶ Setting up a hill-running schedule

. . . .

Every June, runners gather for a race in New Hampshire that some participants jokingly describe as easy because there's just one hill. However, this one "hill" happens to be Mount Washington, the highest peak in New England, and the race course winds up and up and up — for more than 7 miles. This switchback course finishes on the lunar-like, often cloud-shrouded summit.

Certainly, you don't have to take on the Mount Washington Road Race (or, for true diehards, the Pikes Peak Marathon staged near Colorado Springs each summer). And "Climb Every Mountain" doesn't need to become your running theme song. However, even the most moderate hill training can make your leg muscles (quadriceps and gluts) stronger and tougher and increase your enjoyment of running. Because running up hills requires your heart to work harder, it's also a perfect way to improve your endurance. The mental rewards are potentially great, too. When you become confident and more efficient on the hills, you may prefer the ups and downs to puttering about on the flats.

Think Small — At First!

Introduce hill running to your exercise routine in small doses, gradually weaving the ups and downs into your training program. After you feel confident that you can run 20 to 30 minutes at a relaxed pace on a pancake-flat course, then try a course of similar length that includes three or four gradual hills. Even a hill of 5 percent grade is bordering on steep, so break in on very gradual inclines. A small hill that takes you 1 to 2 minutes to reach the top, at a steady but comfortable pace, is about right.

Because you are introducing a brand-new element into your training regimen, you may find yourself out of breath on the inclines. That's because the effort of running up even a gradual hill at a moderate pace can demand the same heart rate as running a fast sprint on the flats. If you need a walk break at the top during those initial hill sessions, that's okay. (However, your eventual goal is to carry all your hard effort into the flat or descent.)

If you really want to ease into hill training, take a hike. That's not an insult; it's just good common sense. Find a path through a state park or along a lake and jog the flat sections. When you reach a slight uphill, walk that part briskly. Then the next time out, try to jog the easier uphills and walk the "killers."

How often should you take on the hills? Once a week is fine at the start. As you improve, you may tour over relatively hilly courses on your regular distance runs, without even thinking about it.

Form First

As you encounter a hill on a run, try to spread your effort out over the entire length of the ascent. Don't try to attack the hill in a furious sprint (although top racers do develop this skill) from the very base of the hill — the hill is a lot bigger than you are! Instead, settle into a steady, smooth pace. If you feel good as you near the very top, you can always pick up your pace.

An active, rhythmic arm swing is crucial for proper hill running. Carry your arms at approximately waist level, keeping an angle in your elbow. Your hands should brush lightly past your hip as your arm swings back, and they should swing up to about chest level when they come forward again. If your hands are coming all the way to about your chin on the forward swing, then you are putting forth an inordinate amount of effort. On very steep grades, however, too much arm activity is always preferable to not enough.

Keep your body posture straight up and down so that your shoulder, chest, and hips are virtually in a straight line, as shown in Figure 9-1. Avoid looking directly down at your feet or hunching your shoulders; both of these habits will inhibit the full extent of your breathing. Your chest should be thrusting up and out.

Relax your neck and shoulder muscles. Don't clench your fists. Keep your hands gently cupped, just as when you're running on flat terrain.

Figure 9-1:
Keep your back straight and your eyes forward when running uphill.

Look almost straight ahead (or ever so slightly down) but don't fix your eyes on the top of the hill. On really long hills, you may want to check your progress with a quick glance to the top, but not every other second.

Hill training is often more of a mental challenge than a physical one. When you first get a hill in sight, look at the top of it only once. Then imagine yourself at the bottom of the other side. If you don't focus solely on how far it is to the top, running the hill won't seem as long or as hard. Always think positive thoughts, and you'll be able to run the entire hill.

Overstriding is a common mistake committed by the novice hill runner. A short, efficient stride will get you to the top with less stress, much in the same way that Tour de France cyclists downshift to gears with the least resistance to ascend those mountain passes in the Alps. The steeper or longer the hill, the more you should downshift to a shorter stride.

You may be surprised to find out that baby steps are the way to climb a very steep hill. Don't worry about speed; just keep moving, and you'll reach the top. Concentrate on quicker strides and more of them, not long strides. Pretend that you're a child again, running up to the second floor of a house and making sure that your feet hit every step.

Here's a checklist to make sure that you're in good form when running on hills:

- ✔ You should notice a very slight, brisk knee-lifting action. This should not be an exaggerated knee lift. You're not a drum major!
- ✔ Strive for a good push off with the toes after foot strike to launch into your next stride.
- ✔ You'll feel a quick flick of the heel and ankle as your leg swings back during that phase of your stride pattern.

Gravity's Rainbow: Going Downhill

After reaching the top of the hill, carry your momentum over the top of the hill and into the subsequent downhill if at all possible. Now gravity is on your side, helping you! The biggest boost will be in your breathing. To state the obvious: You need a lot more oxygen to run up a hill than down a hill. When you're running up a hill, your heart rate might push beyond the range of 170 to 180 beats per minute. But coming down the other side, your heart rate might plunge down to the 130-beats range or less.

However, downhill running can still be hard on your legs, sometimes even harder than running uphill. Be wary of overstriding as you come down. Lean slightly with the slope of the hill, as shown in Figure 9-2. If you constantly look forward and get a clear view of your foot reaching out before you, then you are overstriding, which you don't want to do!

Although you don't want to pound down the hill, you don't want to have your brakes on all the way down either. Of the two techniques, braking is usually the more common problem among novice runners. If you feel a braking action, then you are landing back on your heels too much, which is often a by-product of overstriding. Too much braking on the downhill side not only slows you down and disrupts your natural running motion but also can result in sore leg muscles or even a sore back.

Seek out soft surfaces, preferably a path or nicely cropped grass, for your hill sessions. You'll save a lot of wear and tear on your body, especially on steep downhills, if you avoid concrete sidewalks. Do scout out the terrain ahead of the hill session to avoid any ankle-twisting trouble spots, such as a woodchuck hole or a rocky gully that's hidden by grass.

Try to land on the ball of your foot, or your midfoot, when running downhill, allowing a very slight bend at the knee upon impact. Landing hard on the heel — and with a locked, straight leg — increases the shock to your body.

Figure 9-2: Good downhill form.

You know you've got the form right when you feel like you're flowing down the hill.

If you feel a bit out of control on a plunging descent, opt for a lower and slightly wider arm carriage. Hold your arms out an inch or so more than normal — at about waist level — to improve your balance.

How to Practice Hills

After your initial introduction to running some small hills during regular slow-distance days, you may decide to take on some more challenging hill workouts.

A session of *repeat hills* basically means that you run up to the top of a hill and then jog down (or walk down, if you are a beginning runner). Hills are like pancakes — don't stack too many on your plate until you have a feel for what you can readily digest. In your first session of repeats, start with two or three hills that you can climb in 30 seconds to 1 minute and then add on. Aim for feeling slightly tired but invigorated from the session, just as you would feel after any new workout. If you have to crawl to the car or you're too sore to walk down the stairs the next morning, then you've obviously tackled too many hills at a pace that's too fast. However, if you handled your initial hill sessions with relative ease, then you can gradually increase the number of hill repeats — or pick on a slightly longer or steeper grade — after two or three more workouts on your break-in hill.

Tune into pace

Unless you are a very advanced runner with racing goals, you should never put forth an all-out effort for a hill workout. It's normal to be breathing relatively hard, but you should not be collapsing in an oxygen-starved heap at the top of the hill, and your heart shouldn't feel like a small animal trying to break out of its cage!

Some running coaches and top-notch runners talk about *perceived effort*. Here's how perceived effort (PE) works: Think about effort on a scale from 1 to 10. If 1 on the P.E. scale is a brisk walk pace, then 5 is an easy jog/run pace (similar to talk test pace — a pace that allows you to talk with a training partner while you run), and 10 is all-out, collapse-at-the-finish-line race pace. Based on this scale, you may want to shoot for a 7 or 8 effort when you take on a hill session.

The pace of a repeat hill workout should be a bit faster than the pace you use to get up the hills that you encounter on your regular easy distance runs. But don't try to muscle your way up the hill; finesse, not brute force, is the way to go. Imagine that you're attempting to sneak up the hill before it realizes you're on it!

Your breathing should be almost totally recovered before you run up the hill again. The "talk test" is definitely in order here. If your training partner says, "Let's go get another one!" and you have to reply with sign language and nods of the head, then you aren't ready for the rerun.

Putting it all together

When you feel comfortable handling a session of three or four uphills, try adding some occasional combinations — uphills and downhills together. Remember to carry your momentum over the top of the hill and into the downhill. Perhaps the whole up-and-down path (a loop course works best for this workout) may take you 3 or 4 minutes. Then jog (or walk some, if you must) for a few minutes of recovery and try the loop again.

The difference between running hill combinations and only running the uphill hard (then jogging down again for recovery) is "combos" are good practice for racing. When you encounter hills in a race, your best results will come when you can carry your hard effort up the hill, across the top of the hill, and into the descent — without slacking off your pace.

Flatlander's dilemma

How you can run hills if you live in a flat area like central Florida or parts of the midwestern United States or Canada? Be creative. Flatland runners can use multideck parking garage ramps, highway overpasses, and big, hump-backed bridges to train for a hilly marathon out of town. (But be aware that running in a parking garage may require permission and increased safety awareness.) And don't forget that most of the newest treadmills can provide enough of a percent incline (and descent, too) to please a mountain goat.

Is thar gold in them thar hills?

Speaking in endurance terms, the answer is a resounding "yes!" Whether on the treadmill or straight up a ski slope, hills can get you in shape in rapid order. Hill sessions test your body and mind.

In addition, running up hills is great practice for improving your overall running form. For example, more than a few novice runners fail to keep a consistent, rhythmic arm swing action. But when those same runners take on some uphills, their arm action usually improves simply because they're forced to swing their arms to overcome the resistance of the hill.

Hills also are an excellent transition workout between easy jogging and the fast running (perhaps speed sessions on a flat track) that can get you ready to step up to racing, or simply faster running on your own. Hills are a bit like speed work in disguise; you get strong and fast at the same time. Even though you don't feel like you're moving particularly fast, your heart and muscles are getting a real test.

Arthur Lydiard, a famous Olympic coach from New Zealand, used to train his world-class runners on a 22-mile mountain loop. The hardest part of Lydiard's course ended with a wickedly twisting, rising section that his charges dubbed "the Devil's elbow." You need not confront such evil climbs; but even a moderate weekly hill session will pay heavenly dividends for all aspects of your running program.

Chapter 10

Running in the Elements

· ·

In This Chapter

▶ Facing the cold

▶ Running when the heat is on

▶ Running in the rain

▶ Taking your run to new heights

▶ Dealing with allergies

▶ Avoiding pollution

· ·

Running through the seasons — be it the gently falling flakes of winter's first storm or a sweltering day at the beach — is adventureous and fun. But running outside in the elements also requires a runner to think before bolting out the front door to log a few miles through his or her natural surroundings.

The biggest weather myth about running just may be the one that your Great Aunt Martha perpetuates and swears is true. You know the one. The temperatures have dipped to, oh, perhaps 20 degrees, and Aunt Martha insists that any outside exercise lasting longer than a walk to the mailbox will freeze your lungs.

Winter running can pose some risks. You could slip on an icy sidewalk. You could suffer frostbite to your fingers, nose, toes, ears, and, yes, (no need to discuss this with Aunt Martha . . .) even your private parts if you don't take the necessary precautions. But your lungs probably won't freeze, because producing inner heat is one thing that a revved-up runner's body does fairly well.

Summer months appear to be more runner-friendly, but when the temperatures soar toward 90 degrees and the humidity hovers near 70 percent or above, unprepared runners can suddenly find themselves in danger of dehydration or even heatstroke.

Outdoor runners may also encounter high altitudes, high pollen counts, or high pollution.

Most runners somehow find a way to adapt to these various conditions so that they can stick to their fitness schedule. This chapter offers some suggestions about how to keep on running, no matter what the outdoor conditions are.

The weather is something you have no control over, but you can prepare for it. I think it's important to train in all sorts of weather because you never know what the conditions might be like on race day. Mentally, you want to be prepared for anything.

Out in the Cold

Runners in places like International Falls, Minnesota; Thunder Bay, Ontario; and Fairbanks, Alaska, are well aware that you can run in the cold. If you dress for the occasion, you can brave those subzero temperatures and even enjoy those days in the 20-degree range.

Lay it on me!

Layering your clothing is the Number 1 rule for winter running. Layers help keep in more heat. A synthetic material such as polypropylene, Drylete, or Thermax is a good choice for the layer next to your skin. Don't go for cotton as the bottom layer because cotton holds moisture. For the middle layer, wear a thin turtleneck that's either all synthetic or part cotton/part synthetic materials.

For the outside layer, a nylon windbreaker did the job early in the first running boom (circa 1970), but more breathable material is on the market as the new millennium approaches. On really frigid (or wet and cold) days, with temperatures dipping to 20 degrees or lower, garments such as Gore-Tex outerwear offer heavy-duty cold protection.

Some other materials to consider when shopping for cold weather running gear include Drylete, Ultrex, Moss-Tex, Activent, Lycra, Pro-Core, Supplex, Phin-Tech, and Hydromove (among others). Such "breathable" fabrics offer protections from wind, cold, and wetness.

Running specialty shops are helpful not only when you're looking for shoes. A top-notch running store, staffed by runners, will also have the latest information on the best new gear for running in the elements.

Here are some other items to include in your winter running wardrobe:

- ✔ **Hat:** Most of your body heat will attempt to escape from the head, so wear a knit ski hat, preferably one made of wool or a new-age fabric to maintain the warmth. Wear a hat that covers your ears. On the bitterest of days — those plunging down into the single digits — consider a ski mask, the kind that leaves slits for the eyes, nose, and mouth but covers the rest of the face.

- ✔ **Gloves:** On the coldest days, protect your hands with top-quality ski gloves and a pair of synthetic liners underneath. Thermax is a good glove material that helps keep a runner's hands warm. Are mittens better than gloves? Some runners think so; curling your fingers together inside may keep them warmer. If you can't make up your mind, there are some products — one is called "glittens" — that can be worn as gloves, or easily adapted to mittens on big chill days.

- ✔ **Socks:** To guard against frostbite, wear two pairs of socks, a thin synthetic pair as the first layer, with a wool or part-cotton pair over the top. Don't wear 100-percent cotton socks. Cotton absorbs too much water. Orlon or acrylic fabrics can *wick* (a word that marketers of running fabrics like to use) away moisture and keep your feet dry. And dry feet not only stay warmer but are less likely to suffer blisters.

- ✔ **Neckwear:** It's your neck, so remember to wear either a scarf, neck gaiter, turtleneck sweater, or a jacket featuring a zip-up collar and hood.

- ✔ **Men-only gear:** To protect yourself from Jack Frost's indiscriminate nipping on totally freezing days, consider windbriefs, tight Lycra shorts, or tights, with heavy-duty warm-up pants (made of Gore-Tex fabric) as your outer defense.

- ✔ **Sun protection:** Don't forget sunglasses and sunblock on bright, sunny days, especially if the countryside is blanketed with the white stuff. Rays reflecting off fields of snow can cause sunburn and vision problems.

Too hot to trot? Sometimes runners do overdress and experience "meltdown" in the winter. Ideally, you want to be coolly invigorated when you start your run and just nice and toasty at the end. Keep in mind that your body will heat up to about 20 degrees warmer (than the current air temperature) as you get into the middle of your run.

A sweaty runner can feel cold and miserable on even a 32-degree day if a 20-mile-per-hour wind is blowing, too. That's what the weather folks call the *wind chill factor.* (In this example, the wind chill effect would make it feel about 5 degrees!) To reduce the effect, plan your training run into the wind on the way out and then get a nice push from the gusts on the return home. After you've stoked up a good sweat, you'll feel a lot warmer with the wind at your back.

Before you step out

To set up a safe and successful winter training run, make some preparation before you even leave the house. Start with dry clothing, including shoes. If your running shoes get wet from slush and snow during a run, stuff them with newspaper (to absorb moisture) and put them near (but not directly against) a heat source to dry out for your next training run. Better yet, alternate two pairs of running shoes during foul-weather months.

Muscles take longer to get warm in very cold conditions, so take some extra time to stretch before you venture out on extremely frigid days. You can also jog for several minutes inside if it helps you get your muscles warm before stretching or before you begin your outside training run. If you still feel a bit tight when you start outside, stick to a slow pace until your muscles begin to get loose. See Chapter 8 for info on warming up and stretching.

Try to run during the warmest part of the day, typically between 10 a.m. and 2 p.m. You may have to skip lunch for a 20-minute noontime jaunt, but the daylight hours offer higher temperatures and better visibility for runners.

Because extra winter running gear will induce lots of sweating, dehydration can be a sneaky problem on a winter day. Drink plenty of water before a workout and save the hot drinks, such as coffee and tea, for the post-run fire. But also rehydrate with water after your run, because caffeine drinks can lead to overall fluid loss.

Hazards of the road and sidewalk

All the elements that make running in winter more difficult are at least equally troublesome for drivers. You have less traction on icy, snowy surfaces, and so do people behind the wheel. You don't see as well in a sleet storm (especially through the slits in your ski mask), and drivers don't see as well with the wipers going at full tilt in an attempt to keep the windshield clear.

With that in mind, pay extra attention to vehicles. Expect that they may slide through a stop sign or spin out while making a turn. The sidewalks may be snow-covered or icy, but even a slippery sidewalk is safer than a plowed road with no shoulder. Run against traffic so that you can see what's coming. Be prepared to flop in a roadside snowbank on occasion, if that's what you need to do to avoid getting hit.

Be prepared to run slow when surface conditions are hazardous. If you are hitting occasional icy patches, forget your regular running style and go with a shuffle. If you're going to fall, try to land on your rump, which will be more padded than normal because you're probably wearing several layers of clothing. Do not attempt to break your fall with your hands.

Training partners are good any time of year, but perhaps they are even more valuable in bad-weather months. On those days when you may be tempted to stretch out on the couch and watch reruns of *Baywatch,* a training partner can help get you out the door. More importantly, having an extra pair of eyes never hurts when you're running in traffic, particularly if the vehicles are hampered by bad road conditions. Also, when you're running into a stiff winter wind, try a strategy that cyclists use frequently: Switch off the lead. One runner can break the wind, while the second runner "drafts," saving both energy and body warmth.

To increase your visibility, especially on those late winter afternoons when the light is fading fast, opt for running gear that features reflective safety strips and light clothing. But don't wear all-white clothing if you're running through snowy terrain. Also, if possible, plan your route down roads with streetlights.

For safe running in the dark, the In-Sport illumiNITE jacket has microscopic reflectors in the weave of its fabric. That kind of product can make you glow like Tom Edison's lightbulb.

On thin ice

During winter runs, think twice before crossing lakes, ponds, or rivers that you assume to be frozen solid. You may be dressed warm enough to survive life at the North Pole, but if you fall into cold, icy water, you'll still be at major risk for *hypothermia.* The signs of hypothermia include uncontrolled shivering and disorientation. Hypothermia can occur when your core body temperature plunges below 90 degrees. In such cases, seek heat sources, dry clothes, and hot fluids as soon as possible.

Know when to say when

Despite all your preparations, on certain days, the weather just isn't safe for runners. If the roads are better suited for National Hockey League action, then you might concede a day of outside running and jump on the treadmill or a stationary bike. Or if a blanket of fresh snow has just fallen and the road crews are slow on the job, head to a nearby park for a stint on cross-country skis or snowshoes.

If you do have signs of frostbite — exposed red skin and a numb, tingling, perhaps even a hard-to-the-touch, feeling — do *not* rub the area with snow or ice. Instead, get to a warm, dry environment and *gradually* warm up the cold injured area with warm, not hot, water.

When It's Hot, Play It Cool

Running in sleet, hard rain, or several feet of snow may not be the most enjoyable miles you'll ever tread. But running in the heat — especially pushing hard in it — is what can get novice runners, and even fleet-footed elite racers, in serious trouble.

Just as with winter running, pre-run preparation on hot and/or humid days not only can save you lots of trouble but also can save your life. Runners can gradually become dehydrated over a span of a few days, usually due to inadequate fluid intake after workouts. Losing a half-pint here and a half-pint there can easily happen, and then a really hot day comes along and knocks the runner for an unexpected loop. Runners need proper hydration on a consistent, daily basis, not only on the days that are hot enough to bubble tar on the roads. In order to keep your fluid levels high for running, drink 5 to 8 ounces of water per hour throughout the day.

When it's a real scorcher out there, plan a "water fountain run." If you normally run for an hour, consider splitting the run into three 20-minute sessions — each with a short but refreshing pit stop at a water source. Or better yet, make your final destination a pool or a lake and cool down with a quick dip.

Sweatin' it out

The average runner can lose 2 or 3 pounds of water weight on a warm day, even while running at a comfortable pace. Every pound lost while running represents about a pint of lost fluid that your body needs to replenish. Running at a faster pace can pump out even more of what's arguably your body's most important nutrient.

Not that sweating is bad: That's the way your system keeps a working body cool. In fact, fit runners will sweat more efficiently than beginners attempting to get in shape. Almost all your water loss occurs on the skin's surface, but runners also lose a small percentage — less than 10 percent — through the breathing process.

Be careful on warm, breezy days. The wind helps you feel cooler, but it also accelerates the evaporation of sweat on your skin. The end result is that you may be less aware that you are losing a lot of water.

Bigger runners tend to sweat more than smaller runners, and genetics also can determine your rate of sweating.

How can you tell if your hydration levels are good? A simple (if less than pleasant) way is to check your urine. If it's clear, then you are doing a good job. If it's a dark yellow, or the amount seems scant, then you definitely need to tank up with some H_2O.

Training in hot weather

The body can adapt to many stresses, but it takes time. To acclimatize to heat, start with very modest runs, perhaps as little as 10 minutes. Then gradually add on to the length of these sessions as the summer — and your ability to stand the heat — progresses. Some advanced runners purposely wear extra clothing on mild spring days to help their body adapt to the upcoming hot summer sessions, but that approach may be an extreme strategy for a beginning runner.

Here are some other tips for training in the heat:

✔ Dawn is usually the coolest part of the day, so even if you aren't a morning person, you may want to try running then. Some experienced runners enjoy running at night, but keep in mind that running in the dark presents other potential safety problems.

✔ In addition to a route with plenty of water sources, choose a course with shade and limit your exposure to direct sunlight.

✔ Wear light-colored (preferably white), lightweight, breathable clothing that will reflect the sun's rays. CoolMax and other polyester fabrics are good choices.

✔ Go with a headband to prevent stinging, salty drops of perspiration from getting in your eyes.

✔ No matter how much weight you may want to drop, *never* run in a rubber sweat suit on a warm day (or any day, for that matter). Don't wear a heavy cotton sweat suit either. You won't cut much long-term poundage (it's mostly water weight loss) by wearing such attire, but you can risk serious heat injury.

✔ Be flexible! If you have a hard run scheduled and it turns out to be a "dog day," then put the session off until the weather conditions are more reasonable.

✔ Speaking of dog days, if you run with a canine friend, remember his or her water needs. Panting is not the most efficient way to get rid of heat, and dogs don't sweat. And they can't just whip off that fur coat! Run them by a cool creek and let them do the doggy dive.

A runner who pushes the pace on a warm day can achieve a body temperature of 100 degrees. The risk of heatstroke kicks in around 105 degrees. According to some sports performance studies, runners who drink lots of fluids during a hard effort have a temperature that's several degrees lower than those runners who don't drink fluids.

Racing in the heat

On the day of the 1969 Boston Marathon, the mercury soared to 97 degrees. That particular edition of America's most famous footrace was aptly nicknamed "The Run for the Hoses" because fans along the course came out to soak the runners with garden hoses to keep them cool.

Racing in the heat presents even more problems than *training* in the hot stuff. Competitive urges may tempt you to stick to a time goal that's more suited for cooler temperatures. But unless you are a world-class runner competing for a living, caution should be your guide if race day dawns with conditions more favorable for a 4th of July cookout.

Here are some tips for hot-weather racing:

- ✔ Beware of the "triple-H" factor: heat, humidity, and hills. These conditions on the same course will tax even super-fit runners. Peel back your time goals accordingly, especially for longer races of 10-K to the marathon. Start conservatively and then pick up the pace late in the race if you still feel good.

- ✔ Drink early! If you wait until you feel thirsty, that's already too late. Even some experienced runners tend to scoot by the water stops in the early miles, only to dehydrate a few miles down the road.

- ✔ It's okay to dump some water on your head, although the main benefit is likely to be psychological: A cup of cold water on your head won't impact your overall core body temperature. But make sure that you drink a cup before pouring it on your head!

- ✔ To make sure that you handle the cups at the water station with efficiency, don't try to grab them. Instead, pinch the top of the cup. You'll rarely drop a cup with this method, and the pinching forms a nice funnel that makes it easier to drink.

- ✔ Okay, you finished, and your first inclination may be to hoist a few post-race beers in celebration. But drink water first! Your body is crying out to be rehydrated. Similarly, a sugary drink can give your plunging blood sugar a boost, but follow up with a water chaser.

Danger zone

Despite taking all the right precautions, runners can still fall victim to the heat. A runner who stops sweating, experiences chills, becomes disoriented or dizzy, and is vomiting or has muscle cramping is probably suffering from serious heat injury. A person with these symptoms needs to stop running immediately and take in fluids. In extreme cases, the runner will need qualified medical attention as soon as possible.

Don't let the sun catch you frying

Strong sun not only produces heat that can hurt overall running performance, but it also emits ultraviolet rays that can cause skin cancer. Runners are often exposed to the sun on a fairly regular basis, so sunscreen and sports shades are two weapons that runners should carry in their training bag. When shopping for sunscreen, look for a product that offers at least an SPF of 15.

To reduce rays on the face, some runners like to wear a billed cap. Wearing a cap is certainly effective, but on the hottest days, it may hold in body heat that's attempting to escape through your head. You can compromise by taking the hat off while running through shaded areas (tuck it in the back of your running shorts) and then putting it back on for the sun-drenched miles.

Rainy Day Runners

A guy who has run 20 Boston Marathons was once asked, "Don't you feel like skipping a day when it's raining?" The old road warrior replied, "If you start skipping runs because the weather's too lousy, pretty soon you start missing runs because the weather's too nice!"

A little rain won't hurt a runner. In fact, when trudging along on a hot August evening, you might even welcome a few drops — be those from a friendly cloud or a neighbor's automatic sprinkler.

However, remember that rainy weather — especially downpours — does put a runner more at risk on roads and highways. Vehicle windshields steam up and hamper visibility, and a braking car takes longer to stop on wet pavement. And keep in mind that the average driver doesn't expect anyone to be out running in the rain.

Remember that a summer rainstorm often means thunder and lightning. See Chapter 11 for some advice on what to do if you get caught in a thunderstorm.

If you expect rain on race day, bring along a large plastic garbage bag and an old baseball cap. Wear the bag to the starting line to keep yourself dry in that 20-minute lull before the actual start. You can always toss the bag to the side a minute or so before the starting pistol is raised.

High in the Sky

Suppose that you suddenly are sent to Denver, Colorado, or Saint Moritz, Switzerland, on a business trip. Your running program has been going well, and you don't want to miss many days while you are away. But both of these places are located at high altitudes.

You'll find it harder to run at high altitudes because less oxygen is available for your lungs to suck in. Consider running at "talk test" pace and perhaps not quite as long. You may want to take an occasional day off. When you find yourself thrust into a different training environment, it's often a good strategy to slightly reduce your workout load. If you plan to be at high altitudes for several weeks, then your body will gradually adapt, and you can — very slowly — increase your training effort.

You also need to take extra care to protect yourself from the sun's rays and dehydration at higher elevations. Drink, drink, drink — water that is! And slather on the sunscreen and wear your shades.

Traveling on airplanes tends to dry you out, too. If you do a lot of flying, go for the bottled water as opposed to coffee, tea, caffeine-laced soft drinks, or alcohol, which are all diuretics. *Diuretics* make you lose fluids through increased urination.

Nothing to Sneeze At

Unfortunately, the elements that runners deal with are not limited to soft, falling snowflakes or rays of the sun. Runners who suffer from allergies are only too well aware of nature's other dangers.

What can you do if you have allergy problems?

- ✔ Check in with the Weather Channel or your newspaper and find out the pollen counts. If the reading is very high and your congested nose and watery eyes confirm that fact, cut back on your running until conditions improve.

- ✔ Do your harder runs in the late afternoon or in the evening, when pollen counts tend to be lower.

- ✔ Welcome the rain. The rain has a cleansing effect on the air.

Pollution Solution?

Runners in urban areas not only have to contend with traffic but also with the stuff that traffic spews out: polluting exhaust fumes, such as carbon monoxide. Ozone, another pollutant, comes from the sun's rays reacting with auto exhaust. Runners may complain of itchy, watery eyes — and in extreme cases, a wheezing rasp — as a result of ozone pollution.

Breathing air with 50 ppm (parts per million) of carbon monoxide (average vehicle traffic moving on a street) may cause a slight drop in your running performance. But traffic backed up at a stoplight during rush hour can pump out levels more than twice that amount, causing lightheadedness, coughing, and even chest pains.

Short of training in a gas mask, the inner-city runner should take the following precautions:

- ✔ Avoid running during peak traffic hours.

- ✔ Run as far back from the roadway as possible.

- ✔ Consider indoor exercise alternatives on hot summer days when the weather gurus tell you that the ozone levels are potentially hazardous to your health.

- ✔ Get out of town. If you need an excuse to head for the country, running is as good as any!

Chapter 11

Safety First

● ●

In This Chapter

▶ Protecting yourself from attack

▶ Running with (or away from) dogs

▶ Escaping lightning strikes

▶ Exploring new territory

● ●

*I*n 1988, New York City, a place not easily shaken, was rocked by the brutal rape of a young woman who was running alone one night in Central Park. The story of the so-called Central Park jogger — her attack, the investigation, and the trial of the young men who attacked her — was big news, and it spotlighted the potential dangers of women running alone in the big city.

Although isolated attacks still occur there, the response of the city and the local running community eventually made Central Park a much safer place to run. The New York Road Runners Club established safety patrols and partner programs for women. There was greater cooperation between police and citizens. Runners became more vigilant and better educated on safety procedures. The trend spread across the country, as the Road Runners Club of America (RRCA) took a leading role in educating runners on how to pursue their sport safely; the club produced safety videos and posters and offered self-defense classes for women runners.

So why do runners ignore the most basic safety procedures? Why were about 40 crimes reported against women runners in the Washington, D.C., area alone in 1997, according to the RRCA? Why, a decade after the Central Park jogger, are we still reading tragic stories about women runners?

Not all of these crimes could have been prevented, no matter what kind of precautions were taken, of course. But the key message is that some people simply haven't gotten the message. They choose to ignore it or to remain in denial. Or they believe that, because they're not running in the inner city, they're immune to crime. The fact is that although the United States may statistically be a safer place at the end of the 1990s than it was at the beginning, all runners — not just women — are still potential targets.

And criminals don't pose the only problem. Far more common than an attack on a jogger is the death or injury of a runner hit by a car, usually at night. Runners are also struck by lightning, bitten by dogs, or even, as in one horrifying and highly publicized case in California a few years ago, killed by wild animals.

This chapter isn't meant to scare you: The vast majority of runners pursue the sport for decades without ever running into a problem. But we do want to alert you to some of the potential dangers of our sport and how to avoid them.

So please, don't skip these next few pages just because you think it could never happen to you.

Rules for Running Safely

Most running safety rules are just common sense. But we see so many runners — male and female — who violate them every day that we're including them here just to make sure that you can't say we didn't warn you:

✔ Don't wear headsets. This is the Number 1 rule for safe running. Why? Because when you listen to music or the radio while running outside, you can't hear car horns, cyclists, or, heaven forbid, the footsteps of someone coming up behind you.

"But I love to listen to my music!" is a common rejoinder from those who refuse to give up their headsets. Fine. Wear them when you're running on a treadmill. But when you're outside, especially when you're on the roads, you are simply asking for trouble if you tune out your surroundings. If you need distractions, tune into the sound of the environment around you instead. Or listen to your music at home while you warm up, and play it back internally as you run. Or enjoy the conversation of other runners.

✔ Run against traffic. A bicycle is considered a vehicle, so it is subject to the same laws as cars and trucks. Cyclists ride with traffic. You are not a vehicle. You are a runner. You are also in a highly vulnerable position if you're running near cars, trucks, and bicycles. So the best way to prevent an untimely meeting with one of these vehicles is to be able to see them. That means running on the side of the road or on the sidewalk and running while facing traffic.

✔ If you run at night, make yourself visible. Wear light-colored clothing and invest a few dollars in a reflective vest, which you can purchase at a local running store or through a mail-order running catalog.

✔ Don't challenge cars to a race. If you and a car are both approaching an intersection, stop and let the car go first. (News flash: They're faster than you.)

✔ Beware of stopped cars waiting to make a right turn. Stop and wait until they make the turn, or run behind them.

✔ Run with others. This may be the easiest way to avoid problems altogether. Sharing the road with other runners is also a great way to stay motivated and to enjoy the sport. You can find potential partners through your running club, your running apparel store, or community bulletin boards at your library.

 If you must run alone, a treadmill at home or at a health club is a much safer option. A local track also offers some protection, but not if you're running alone and after dark.

✔ Avoid running alone in unpopulated, unfamiliar areas and stay away from trails surrounded by heavy brush.

✔ Do not wear jewelry. But do carry identification or write your name, phone number, and blood type on the inside sole of your running shoe.

✔ Always trust your intuition. If you're unsure about a person or a place, avoid it.

✔ Carry a noisemaker or get training in self-defense and the use of pepper spray. And always call police if something happens to you or someone else or if you see something or someone suspicious.

✔ Don't stop to give directions to strangers in cars if you are running alone.

Encountering Loose Dogs

Dogs share the roads with runners. Usually, they're friendly, leashed, under the watchful eye of a master, and having a grand old time. Sometimes, they're none of these things.

Should you come across a dog on the loose while you run, stay cool. If the dog doesn't see you coming, announce yourself from a distance. Say something like "What a good dog!" If the dog responds with a wag of the tail, chances are, you're okay. If the answer is a baring of teeth or a belligerent, what-are-you-doing-on-my-turf? growl, find another way around this pooch.

If you're in a position where you still have to run past the dog, keep your distance. "If the dog comes forward and threatens you, face the dog and make aggressive noises," advises Trevor Smith of the American Running and Fitness Association. "Clap your hands loudly and shout 'No!' or 'Sit.' Many house pets really are not very brave and can be intimidated quite easily, especially if you behave in what they perceive to be an erratic, noisy manner. You need to sound aggressive, but don't actually be aggressive."

In general, Smith notes, house pets are friendly (with the occasional exception). You're more likely to encounter aggressive animals in rural areas, where dogs are often kept outdoors and sometimes have hunting instincts. Such animals may chase you, but he says, "They'll usually lose interest if they're ignored."

Running with Your Dog

Maybe it started with Butkus, that big dog who accompanied boxer Rocky Balboa on his memorable training runs in the famous *Rocky* movies. Maybe runners just like the security of having a German shepherd at their side. Maybe pet owners just realize that taking the dog along is a good way for the dog to get some exercise, too.

Whatever the reason, dogs on the run with their masters are a fairly common sight on the roads. It's nice to see. What isn't such a pleasant sight is a dog on a hot day, its paws burnt on the hot road surfaces, panting and obviously thirsty, and yet loyally following its oblivious master.

Dogs should embark on a running program the same way that people do. The first step is to take them to the veterinarian to make sure that the dog is healthy and able to handle the exercise.

Hip problems, which are common among some dogs that run, are usually hereditary. Veterinarian Mark Katz, writing in *Running & FitNews,* says the best way to find a canine running companion is to buy your puppy from a breeder who can certify that both parents are free of hip problems. This certification, he adds, is provided by the Orthopedic Foundation of America, which is affiliated with the Veterinary College of the University of Missouri.

Wait until the puppy is 9 months old before you let him begin regular running. Start slowly and build up gradually, just like *you* need to do. "Start with 5 minutes or runs three times a week for the first couple months and increase the distance slowly," advises David Bebiak, director of Pet Nutrition and Care Research for the Purina Pet Care Center. "If your dog begins to lag behind while you're jogging, slow down or stop to let your pet rest."

"Use a lightweight leash," says Katz, "and train your pet to run close to your left side, reducing the chance of being hit by a car or bike. Don't allow your dog to run unleashed."

In hot weather, exercise the same caution with your dog that you would for yourself:

- ✔ Reduce the amount of time spent exercising.
- ✔ Avoid running at the hottest times of day.
- ✔ Make sure that your dog has plenty of water.
- ✔ Be careful where you run. Hot cement can burn a dog's feet, and running off the roads on rough terrain can cut them.

Treat your dog as well as you do yourself, and you may have a running partner for life. But don't assume that every dog must have its days on the road. Some dogs are better off running around the backyard.

When Lightning Strikes

So you're running along on a warm summer evening, and suddenly . . . Crack! Boom! Lightning flashes, thunder rumbles, and the sky opens up.

The least of your worries here is getting wet. That can actually be pleasant on a warm day. The rain won't kill you, but the lightning could.

Here's what the *Penn State University Sports Medicine Newsletter* suggests for storm safety: At the first sound of distant thunder, take cover. Good places for shelter include wooded areas, an enclosed building, or a vehicle with the windows rolled up. Avoid metal bleachers and goalposts (if you're running on a high school track) or open spaces and isolated trees.

"Seek the forest, not the tree," advises Michale Cherington, M.D., who directs the Lightning Data Center at St. Anthony's Hospital in Denver. "If there are 1,000 trees, the odds of being struck are reduced to 1 in 1,000."

If you're caught outdoors, find a ditch or some other low spot away from trees, fences, and poles. If you're in the woods, seek shelter under low trees and bush.

Finally, the newsletter recommends using the "flash to bang" formula to estimate the distance of the storm. For each 5-second count between the sight of a lightning flash and the sound of thunder, the lightning is 1 mile away. For example, if you hear the thunder 25 seconds after seeing the flash, the lightning is 5 miles away. The longer the "flash to bang," the more time you have. But don't hesitate. Take cover as soon as you can.

Running Away

Running is a traveler-friendly sport. All you need to do is pack your shoes, and off you go.

But be careful where you run. Although exploring new places on the run can be fun, it can also be dangerous.

To ensure a safe run, do a little homework. Call the Road Runners Club of America or visit its Web site to find out about running clubs. Check the running magazines to see whether a race is scheduled for the weekend when you'll be visiting the area. You can also check the www.dadait/rtp Web site, which provides information on running trails. Or as part of a $25 annual membership to the American Running and Fitness Association (www.rrca.org/~rrca/), you are entitled to maps of places to run all over the United States.

At the very least, ask the concierge at the hotel or any runners you see on the local roads about safe and scenic routes in their area.

Your card, please

A few years ago, while on business in Japan, sports agent Arthur Kaminsky went for a run, through the crowded streets of Kyoto. Watching the sights and thinking about his next big deal, Kaminsky forgot to pay attention to where he was going. "Soon, I was lost," he recalled. "All the streets looked the same, and I couldn't find anyone who spoke English."

Kaminsky eventually found his way home . . . and found a way to avoid repeating that same mistake. Here's his tip for running overseas: "Bring along a card from the hotel you're staying at," he says, "preferably one printed in the native language." Pin it to your shorts, and if you get lost and can't find anyone who speaks English, you can show the card to someone who can at least point you in the right direction.

Bon voyage!

Part III
The Competitive Edge

The 5th Wave   By Rich Tennant

In this part . . .

*W*e help you to prepare for racing. Not all runners want to compete, but for those who do, we provide some programs that will help you get in shape for race day. We even offer a simple marathon-training program for those runners ready for such a challenge.

Chapter 12
Advanced Training

- -

In This Chapter

▶ Increasing the miles

▶ Going for speed

▶ Progressing to a higher level

▶ Training on a track

▶ Monitoring your heart

▶ Working out in the proper order

- -

A world-class runner once described training as pulling back a bow to shoot an arrow at a tough-to-hit target. If you pull the bow back just a tiny bit, then the arrow won't have enough "oomph" behind it to even reach the target, never mind hit the bull's-eye. But if you pull the bowstring back with too much force, you might wildly overshoot the target or even snap the bowstring.

The trick in running, of course, is to be somewhere in the middle. Runners who train inconsistently rarely discover their utmost running potential — both in terms of performance and enjoyment. But runners who habitually overtrain greatly increase their risk of injury or mental burnout, and the result may be pure frustration.

Where Are You Headed?

After you begin running more than three or four times a week and your jaunts begin to take more than 30 minutes, then you probably aren't running just for weight loss or lower cholesterol anymore. You may be leaning toward a race. Or perhaps you have already finished a short race — just for fun, at your normal training run pace — and (dare you admit it?) would like to run faster or run longer or simply have more energy in your next competition.

After those initial steps out the door when you first take up running, the next biggest — and most intimidating — step is the step up to racing.

However, the less obvious step (but a very important one) is the step in between fitness running and racing. Call it specific training or quality training or advanced training, but all those terms essentially mean the training that prepares you for harder running and the rigors of racing. In most cases, this training requires an increase in the intensity of some of your workouts and often an increase in overall mileage.

Gradually Adding On the Miles

People breaking out of fitness-jogger mode may be in a hurry to achieve serious-runner status, so they begin to pile on the miles. But resist the temptation to make huge jumps in weekly mileage. Instead, commit yourself to a plan of patient progression.

If you are presently running four days a week and averaging 15 to 20 miles over those four days of training, then you can reasonably add a fifth day of training. But in the same scenario, you are courting injury risk if you jump right to a weekly running program of 40 miles, which is double your previous total.

Similarly, trying to build mileage on a continuous, linear spiral is foolish; like a child's teetering block tower, there's bound to be a downside! Instead, keep your mileage increases in the 5 to 10 percent range, and occasionally retreat to slightly lighter training loads (especially if you are frequently fighting fatigue) before moving up your weekly mileage again.

Commitment to your running program is important, but don't become a slave to your training log. Instead, listen to your body (a pearl of running wisdom at least three decades old!) and let that be your guide. If you're tired, opt for an easy day — or even a day off.

On occasion, retreating from your highest weekly mileage totals is also a wise move. Maybe you've finally worked up to 40 miles of running per week over six days. If you are facing an extremely busy week, with pressing business or family commitments, however, you can drop down to 30 miles spread over five days. Stay flexible with your running; make sure that it works for you and not the other way around!

The Need for Speed

Some novice runners finish a 5-K race and slog through a couple of hour-long runs, and right away they start thinking "marathon!" Resist the temptation. Yes, beginners can complete a marathon; by jogging and walking, jogging and walking, almost anyone can get through 26.2 miles. But for best results at longer distances, beginners should first train for shorter races by increasing their speed and improving their running form.

Speed Training 101

Some novice runners get scared when they hear the term *speedwork*. They get visions of mean-spirited football coaches forcing their players to run wind sprints on a hot August day in preseason camp.

But an introduction to speed training sessions (or other quality sessions such as hill repeats) should be very gradual, and such workouts don't have to hurt. In fact, if you do the initial workouts properly, they *shouldn't* hurt. However, the workouts should be slightly challenging and invigorating.

For your first test of faster running, run on a dirt path or closely cut grass field. Go for a 30-minute run, but three times during the middle of the run, try to pick up the pace for about 30 seconds to 1 minute.

Don't bolt into an all-out sprint. Merely notch up the pace gradually so that it's faster than your usual training pace. After each little surge of speed is over, walk briskly or jog very easily until your breathing becomes comfortable again. If you are doubled over and gasping for breath after each burst of speed, then you are running too fast.

There. That's your first speed session. Basically, you revved up your heart rate a bit, and you probably moved your arms and legs slightly faster. But it counts.

Run on forgiving surfaces, such as dirt paths or grass, and you will save wear and tear on your body and your running shoes. Don't just pound the roads and sidewalks day after day. If you run six days a week, try to do half your workouts, especially some of your fast sessions, on off-road surfaces.

Another simple introductory speed session involves telephone poles. Trees also work well. No, you don't have to climb them! Run alongside a road with a line of telephone poles, starting out at your easy run pace. After you are warmed up, pick up the pace several times during the run by zipping past three or four poles (or trees). Then jog (or walk) until you recover your breathing, and repeat the process.

Always start and end your quality workouts with at least 10 to 15 minutes of easy jogging for warm-up and cool-down purposes. Some light stretching before and/or after also is beneficial. Chapter 8 has more information on warming up and stretching.

Quality time

Quality sessions are any workouts when you are going noticeably faster than a comfortable run pace. Most of your regular distance runs should be done at talk-test level: That is, you should be able to converse with a running partner without gasping on every other word.

Quality runs shouldn't leave you bent over, gasping for oxygen, either, but obviously you should do these workouts at a speed or effort that's faster than talk-test pace.

Here's a grand-slam sampler pack of four basic types of quality workouts:

- ✔ **Fartlek:** This session is basically described in the "Speed Training 101" section. The runner changes speeds occasionally during an easy distance run, working, if you will, different training gears. (If you owned a sports car with five gears, you wouldn't limit yourself to using just two of them, right?)

  Fartlek is a Swedish term meaning speedplay. A fartlek is a way of exploring your different speeds during a training run. Coaches some-times instead use the terms *surges* or *pick-ups* because they tend to draw fewer snickers than *fartleks*.

- ✔ **Hills:** Adding hill workouts can improve both your speed and endurance, force you to use proper running form, build muscle strength, and galva-nize your mental tenacity. A typical quality hill session might consist of jogging 10 or 15 minutes for a warm-up, running up a hill (one that takes at least 30 seconds but probably not more than 3 minutes to climb) at a challenging pace (brisk and smooth), and then jogging back down for a rest. Start with two or three runs up the incline in your debut hill session.

- ✔ **Repeats:** In this workout, you run a certain distance — perhaps one lap around a 400-meter track — and shoot for a certain time. Then, after a short rest break, the runner repeats the distance at a quick, brisk pace again. Runners usually like to run repeats on a track because they can easily monitor both the rate of speed and the distance covered.

- ✔ **Tempo runs:** This workout is also sometimes called a *steady state run.* These are distance runs of a brisk but controlled pace, usually run at a speed about halfway between your warm-up jog pace and race pace. Tempo runs are sandwiched between an easy warm-up and a cool-down jog. The actual tempo portion of the session usually lasts at least 15 minutes, and perhaps as long as 30 minutes for advanced runners.

Tempo run sample workout

If your easy jog pace is 8 minutes per mile and your 5-K race pace is 7 minutes per mile, then your tempo run effort is approximately a 7:30-per-mile pace. A modest tempo run session, then, might consist of 2 miles in a 16-minute warm-up period, immediately followed by 2 miles at tempo run pace (covered in 15 minutes), followed by a 2-mile cool-down in 16 minutes. That totals 47 minutes of running, covering about 6 miles. As you improve, you may want to extend the middle tempo segment to 3 or even 4 miles.

Advancing on All Fronts

After completing the beginner stages of a training program, especially one that follows up with a gradual introduction to quality sessions, almost all runners begin to get in shape. Coaches and exercise physiologists explain (sometimes accompanied by lots of scientific jargon) that the runner's body is being exposed to stress and then adapting to that stress. In the most simplistic terms, you know that you're getting in shape when the 4-mile loop that you struggled through last month suddenly feels much easier.

In the best-case scenarios, you may see improvements in several different areas at once: Your speed, endurance, and running form may all improve simultaneously. You can, almost inexplicably, go farther, faster, and smoother, as if you were an unstoppable army advancing on all fronts!

Few runners feel great every time they go out on a run. However, eventually your good training days will outnumber those days where you slog along and can't wait until it's over. When you reach the point when almost every run is a good one, you're probably ready to increase your training distance or rev up your training speed.

 Never add several new elements to your training in the same one- or two-week period. For example, don't begin a new weight lifting program at the same time that you're increasing your weekly mileage and taking on your first hill session. Instead, gradually introduce new elements over the space of several months, one at a time.

Get on Track

Some runners steer clear of running on a track because they find it too monotonous. ("Running around in circles" is a familiar objection.) Other runners find tracks too intimidating. (You're supposed to be a speed burner if you're running on a track, right?)

However, running on a track, preferably an outdoor one that is 400 meters around, can help enthusiastic rookies advance their fitness levels.

The good thing about conducting a quality session on the track is that you can get constant and accurate feedback. You'll know exactly how fast you are running over an exact distance. On a week-to-week basis, you can easily monitor improvements in your overall running fitness by comparing one track workout to previous speed sessions.

For example, if a runner finishes a two-lap repeat around a standard outdoor track in 4 minutes, then the runner is essentially running an 8-minute-per-mile pace. Perhaps that runner can do only one of these two-lap repeats in his very first track speed session.

But suppose that two months later, after more training, that same runner can run a total of three two-lap repeats in 3 minutes and 30 seconds each, taking appropriate rest breaks after each repeat that is run. Then that runner is getting valuable proof of improvement, both in endurance (the runner can now run a total of three of the two-lap repeats compared to just one in the original session) and speed (the runner is zipping through the two-lap repeats at a much faster pace).

Here's a few tips that should make your first "track test" more fun and productive:

- ✔ If you want to cut down on the running-in-circles feeling that can happen with track running, do your warm-up run and cool-down run away from the track.

- ✔ Be aware of faster runners on the track. Reserve the lane closest to the infield for running the fast parts of your workout. Do your recovery jogs or walks in the outer lanes.

- ✔ If the track's clear, consider switching directions on occasion. Too much running in one direction on a track with tight turns can sometimes cause some nagging aches and pains to your inside leg (the leg closest to the infield). The side of the knee, hip, and ankle get more stress, especially on some smaller, tighter indoor tracks.

- ✔ If you run on a track with lots of other runners, don't get caught up in racing against the first guy or gal who blazes past you. Stick to your own workout plan.

- ✔ Be flexible! Extreme conditions, such as wind, heat, or extreme cold, make it harder to hit your workout times. Adjust your time goals or even shorten the distance of your repeats accordingly.

- ✔ If you are having an off day at the track, you can always turn off your stopwatch and just run at a moderately challenging pace. You can always tackle the timed track session on another day.

On those rare days when you are having a fantastic workout, resist the temptation to add on more miles or more speed. It's better to leave a challenging session feeling good. You can always up the ante the next time out.

Heart of the Matter

One way to monitor your quality sessions is to take your pulse during the rest phase. Typically, an in-shape runner may have a resting heart rate of around 50 to 60 beats per minute. That same in-shape runner's heart rate may go up to between 100 and 120 during the warm-up run prior to a workout. Then, while blasting through parts of a demanding track or hill session, our runner's heart rate may soar to 180. On a controlled tempo run, a typical in-shape runner probably, by definition of a tempo pace, registers a heart rate somewhere in between 130 and 170.

Truly advanced runners (or runners with special health considerations) may want to use a heart monitor to keep tabs on overall effort. An obvious advantage of using a heart monitor is that you don't have to stop your workout to take your heart rate. Instead, you only have to glance down at the wristwatch monitor, which flashes up the information that it gets from the small transmitter strapped across your chest.

Some heart rate monitors are equipped with special alarms that beep when the runner exceeds a certain effort. For example, suppose that a runner plans to hold a tempo-run pace in the 160-beats-a-minute range, but the rate begins to push too hard — into the 170-and-above range in this scenario. A beeping alarm acts as the highway patrolman, essentially saying, "You're speeding, buddy!" Such warnings can be valuable in the fight to avoid overtraining.

When your heart rate returns to about the same level it is at the finish of your warm-up run (for the sample runner just discussed, that would be around 120 beats per minute), then your body is sufficiently recovered to take on another track repeat or conquer another hill.

But you can also opt for the old-fashioned way: Stop and take your pulse. The artery on the side of your neck, just below your jaw, is a good place to take your pulse. You can also get a reading at your temple.

When taking your pulse, try counting for 20 seconds and then multiply by three.

Finding your max

If you really plan to closely monitor your hard training effort, you need to have some idea — at least a ballpark figure — of what your maximum heart rate is. Although there are more precise methods, a simple way to roughly figure out your maximum heart rate is to subtract your age from 220. For example, a 35-year-old runner subtracts 35 from 220 to come up with 185 beats per minute for a maximum heart rate. (This method usually is fairly accurate with fitness runners but less so for advanced, well-trained runners with a great range of heart rates.)

Keep in mind that your maximum heart rate is just a guideline reflecting the upper levels of your very hard efforts. At the end of the day, your maximum heart rate is just a number — not a Holy Grail to reach in a workout to prove that you're putting in the effort.

Talk test

For runners just introducing themselves to advanced training, the talk test (which you can read about in Chapter 4) is still an easy way to judge perceived effort (which we discuss in Chapter 9). That is, simply, don't bolt back into a hard effort until you can jog (or walk briskly) and hold a conversation with your running partner. You don't want your heart rate to crash down so far that you are almost totally recovered. On the other hand, you should not already be breathing hard when you launch into another challenging part of the workout.

A Call for Order

Most runners, after they're bitten with the training/racing bug, are willing to put in the effort. But a willingness to hammer (which means "going hard" in runner's lingo) isn't enough. In fact, too much quality work can hurt your performance. A runner must place workouts in the proper order.

Build your house

Runners can choose from various ways to get in top shape. Most running programs, however, certainly include the methods of Arthur Lydiard. Lydiard was a famed New Zealand coach of a small but fabulous batch of Olympic runners from 1960 to 1970. Almost every system used by long-distance runners today has some components based on his philosophies.

Although the following advice is a greatly simplified overview of Lydiard's methods, here's basically what he advised his runners to do:

✔ **Build a base of mileage.** The base is almost exclusively easy miles — but lots of them — to get the body ready for harder, faster quality sessions. The object is not to blow through your workouts but simply to cover the distance on a consistent basis and avoid injury in the process.

✔ **Run hills,** which is covered in Chapter 9. Keep in mind that even a weekly hill session can pay heavenly dividends in terms of fitness.

✔ Only after a runner has carved out an endurance/strength position (from base mileage and hills) should speedwork, such as track repeats and races, interlaced with plenty of rest, be introduced.

Although Lydiard emphasized months of some of these phases, particularly the base mileage phase, the average runner can still do quite well on a modified Lydiard plan. Start with base mileage, add hills (and tempo runs) in a transition phase, and then sharpen up for the main racing season with speedwork and rest days. The rest days restore energy to your legs and mind. After your most important races are done, recover with a brief period of active rest and some cross-training, such as cycling, weight lifting, cross-country skiing, hiking, or swimming. Then start over at the top by very gradually rebuilding your base mileage again.

In effect, a modified Lydiard method is like building a house: You start with the less-than-exciting task of constructing a solid foundation, which you can compare to the base miles. You then progress to walls and support beams, which are like the hills and tempo runs. You finish with more splendid touches — the speedwork and racing — that make your house stand out.

Coaches also are fond of using the cake-baking analogy when discussing the training process. The ingredients are the base miles, the baking process is the hills, and, finally, the frosting on the cake is the speedwork and racing.

 When discussing training programs, some coaches and runners use the term *periodization.* Periodization refers to the phases of an overall training program in which one particular training method is most emphasized, such as base building, hills, or speedwork.

What's your focus?

When you start to map out a yearly training plan, the distance that you're training for should determine the amount of time that you spend building base mileage or zipping through speed sessions on the track. Someone training for the Boston Marathon will train quite a bit differently than a runner who's gearing up to run a personal-best mile on the track.

There's still some overlap of training sessions no matter what type of goals a runner has. Both marathoners and milers use easy distance runs at the beginning of a training season, for example. At some point, however, you must zero in on the particular demands of the distance. For the marathon, that's covering 26.2 miles over several hours; for the mile, it's zipping through (hopefully) four brisk laps of an outdoor track in a matter of minutes.

A coach can be a big help when you're planning your yearly or even weekly training program. Some running clubs or running specialty stores have coaches who will assist you for a yearly membership fee. You can also tap into some online coaching advice these days; some advice is free, and some is pay-for-hire.

A little R and R

After a runner is properly motivated and focused, the most difficult element of training probably won't be hills, the weekly long run, or even speedwork. Nine times out of ten, the most difficult part of training will be rest!

Runners need to recover, both physically and mentally, from hard workouts and exacting races. That's why it's so important to incorporate active rest phases in your overall yearly training program, particularly if you race one or two marathons in a 12-month span.

The average fitness runner looking to step up to racing can perform quite well with one or (at most) two quality (speed and/or hills) workouts a week. The rest of the week can consist of easy distance runs of various lengths and duration at talk-test pace.

Beware of overtraining

A successful college coach/physiologist was once asked what the most popular method of training among distance runners was these days. The coach quipped, "Overtraining!"

Left to their own devices, many runners do overtrain. But after you've progressed beyond rookie running (meaning that you are already running fit), then you'll have less injury risk and probably better performances if you feel *slightly* undertrained.

Here's how you know whether you might be overtraining:

✔ Your morning pulse rate is suddenly elevated. Suppose that your normal resting pulse rate is 60 to 64. But for the better part of a week, it's up around 70 or 71.

An angel to love, to cherish for life.

My heart, my soul, my best friend, my wife.

—Al Joyner

Florence Griffith Joyner
"Flo-Jo"

December 21, 1959 –
September 21, 1998

1988 Seoul Olympics, 100m. Courtesy of Mike Powell and Allsport

October 10, 1987,
Florence Griffith marries
Al Joyner.

November 13, 1990, Mary Ruth
Joyner is born to proud parents
Florence and Al.

1986 Cologne. Courtesy of Allsport

"I place no limits on what I can do because I know that anything is possible if I believe in myself and work hard."
—Florence Griffith Joyner

1988 U.S. Olympic Trials. Courtesy of Tony Duffy and Allsport

"Even if she had never run a step, it seems likely that we
would have heard of Flo Jo somehow. . . . She was always
driven to be the best, and she had the talent to back that up."
—Jeff Hollobaugh, ESPN SportsZone

"Flo-Jo was loved and admired as a great human being. Her contributions to the humanities will keep the torch burning forever."
—Mal Whitfield, 1948–1952 Olympic Gold Medalist, 800-meter

"Florence Griffith Joyner was one of a kind. She did many different things with style and grace."
—Bert Rosenthal, The Associated Press

"Florence brought a certain style to the track, something so different, with her fashionable appearance and her stunning speed. Her performance in the summer of 1988 was a monumental feat . . . an absolutely monumental feat that will be remembered for decades."
—Patricia Rico, USA Track & Field President

"Florence Griffith Joyner will be remembered among America's greatest Olympians, and she will be recalled with the legends, like Wilma Rudolph and Babe Didrikson Zaharias."
—Bill Hybl, United States Olympic Committee President

1987 World Championships in Rome.
Courtesy of Gray Mortimore and Allsport

*"What has been
proved is that her
individualism did not
prevent her from
sharing with others.
She generously gave
time and money to a
variety of causes
usually associated
with children and
their needs. Florence
Griffith Joyner was a
remarkable American
who lived an
unforgettable life."
—Jay Ambrose,
Scripps Howard*

*"It takes practice and perseverance,
but as long as I hold on to my dreams,
I know they'll become a reality."*
—Florence Griffith Joyner

Courtesy of Tony Duffy and Allsport

1988 Seoul Olympics 4 x 400m. Courtesy of Bob Martin and Allsport

"The beauty of her was that she never changed. She was the same Flo-Jo before [her success], and she was the same Flo-Jo after."
—John Smith, 1968 Olympian

1988 Seoul Olympics, 200m. Courtesy of Tony Duffy and Allsport

"There's a very short list of instantly recognizable female athletes.
Flo-Jo is one of those athletes."
—Bob Williams, *Burns Sports Celebrity*

"I believe in the impossible because no one else does, and that gives me an excellent chance at accomplishing it."
—Florence Griffith Joyner

1988 Soul Olympics, 100m. Courtesy of Russell Cheyne and Allsport

1988 Olympic Trials. Courtesy of Tony Duffy and Allsport

"Visualize yourself accomplishing your goals, and nothing can stop you from achieving them."
—Florence Griffith Joyner

1988 Seoul Olympics. Courtesy of Tony Duffy and Allsport

1988 U.S. Olympic Trials. Courtesy of Allsport

*"When you've trained as best you can and you know your competition has done the same,
nothing really matters but your mental strength and your belief."*
—*Florence Griffith Joyner*

1988 Seoul Olympics. Courtesy of Tony Duffy and Allsport

"She went fast in life. She went too fast from it."
—Gary Shelton, St. Petersburg Times

1988 Soul Olympics, 100m. Courtesy of Steve Powell and Allsport

"In the beginning, she was one of 11 . . .
in the end, she was one of a kind."
—Jim Huber, CNN/Sports Illustrated

"Hold on to your own dreams and never, ever give up."
—*Florence Griffith Joyner*

"Know no limitations."
—*Florence Griffith Joyner*

Records, Medals, and Achievements

100 meters	10:49 July 16, 1988 World Record
200 meters	21:34 September 29, 1988 U.S. Record
1984 Olympic Games	Silver Medal 200 meters
1987 World Championships	Gold Medal 4 x 100 meters Silver Medal 200 meters
1988 Olympic Games	Gold Medal 100 meters 200 meters 4 X 100 Silver Medal 4 X 400
February 25, 1989	Florence Griffith Joyner retires from track and field

Other Achievements and Honors

James E. Sullivan Award for the 1988 Outstanding Amateur Athlete

Associated Press Female Athlete of the Year

United Press International Sportswoman of the Year

Jesse Owens Outstanding Track and Field Athlete

Track and Field Female Athlete of the Year

U.S. Olympic Committee Sportswoman of the Year

Distinguished Service Award from the United Negro College Fund

The Nickelodeon Kid's Choice Award

The People's Choice Award

Appointed co-chair to the President's Council on Physical Fitness (1993)

Inducted into the National Track and Field Hall of Fame (1995)

Spokesperson for the American Cancer Society, The Multiple Sclerosis Foundation, and the Osteoporosis Business Coalition (1995)

Inducted into the Women's Sports Foundation Hall of Fame (1998)

Arete Award for Courage in Sports "Life Award" (1998)

Glamour Magazine's Ten Most Influential Women in History Award (1998)

✔ Your performances in both races and hard workouts have leveled off, or even fallen, even though you feel like you are putting a 100-percent effort into your running.

✔ Normally an energetic runner, you inexplicably don't feel like running for days at a time.

✔ At the start of a training run, your legs feel "dead," or they're always sore and tight.

✔ Your sleeping patterns get weird. Maybe you can't sleep at night (even though you are training harder than ever), but you feel like you can barely stay awake in the late afternoon hours.

✔ Every cold or flu bug that comes down the pike wants to reside in *your* body and hang around for a while.

✔ Normally a nice, happy person, you suddenly have a short fuse and a long face.

✔ You find yourself sneaking out the door at 11 p.m. for a 3-mile run. It's the end of the week and you already have in 47 miles, but you think that 50 will look a lot better in your training-log entry.

✔ You can recall every lap-split run in the recent world record for 10,000 meters, but it takes you a while to come up with the correct names of your three children.

Reach your peak

Although overtraining can be a problem at almost any time, self-sabotaging yourself in the days just before a big race is particularly frustrating.

When runners and coaches talk about peaking, it's not the same thing as scaling the Matterhorn. In running jargon, peaking that's done perfectly can be similarly exhilarating to mountain climbing, however. In the running sense of the word, *peaking* means being in top-notch condition for the most important race of your season. It means being physically prepared, mentally focused, and well rested. When all three of those elusive elements are aligned, then a personal-best performance or time is possible.

Runners can increase their chances of hitting the perfect peak by realizing that training has a delayed effect; that is, a hard workout will not instantly help runners to elevate their fitness level. Sometimes you need weeks for the diligent training you are presently doing to help you get to the next level. You are stressing the body, but the body takes time to adapt to that stress and get ready for another dose.

Conversely, a killer workout done on Monday, a mere five days before a race on Saturday, could leave your legs (and head) less than 100 percent fresh for the fight. Similarly, a lot of extra miles the week of a competition, even those logged at a slow pace, can detract from your race.

Very few runners can be totally sharp for every single competition. So don't even try! Instead, use some early-season races more like time trials that provide feedback on where you are in way of preparation for more important races later in the year.

If you race 10 to 20 times over the span of a year, try to pick out perhaps two or three of the most important races and get some extra rest just before those events so that you can really be at your best.

Getting extra rest doesn't mean that you do nothing but lie around the week of a race. However, you do need to certainly get extra sleep, hydrate well, and reduce your training load and intensity. Because the art of peaking varies from individual to individual, learn from experience and refer to past entries in your training log. After you find the proper formula of run-and-rest that works well for you, stick with it.

Visiting another city for a race is exciting, but don't spend the day before the big competition walking around to see the tourist sites. Stay off your feet and hydrate! Take in the highlights of the city the day *after* the race.

Keep the peak

After world-class runners reach super-fit levels, they can hold a peak for a number of weeks. But eventually even the performances of Olympic greats begin to level off. This phase is often referred to as a *plateau* in the overall training process. Sometimes performances also decline. This decline usually happens slowly, but on occasions, it may occur abruptly.

Whether you're a superstar or a rookie, when your racing or training performances have hit a plateau (or, worse, a sinkhole), then it's time to start over. Begin again with an active rest involving some cross-training, followed by a gradual rebuilding of base mileage. After you have rebuilt a decent base, add transition workouts such as tempo runs and hills, followed by speed sessions and the pursuit of the perfectly peaked race.

Chapter 13

A Day at the Races

Dr. George Sheehan, the late runner/writer/philosopher, once said, "The only difference between a runner and a jogger is an entry blank."

In many different ways, runners who have signed those race entry forms are no longer running (or jogging) exclusively for fitness and fresh air. But don't assume that people race only because they enjoy blood-and-guts competition. Many runners race to socialize, to raise money for a worthy charity, or to simply have an excuse to visit a different part of the world.

Of course, you don't really *have* to run a race, any more than you have to try skydiving. The running world will not reject you because you never toed a starting line. And, despite Sheehan's quip, some runners never pin an official race number to their singlet. Some people run the length of the Appalachian Trail in hiking boots with a 50-pound pack on their back but never enter a race. Other people run for 20 minutes, three times a week, on a health club treadmill and have absolutely no desire to race against fellow human beings or the digital numbers on a plastic wristwatch. And there's not a single thing wrong with a runner's decision not to race.

There's a flip side to the racing issue, however. Racing is such an obvious metaphor for life — with its high hopes, rough spots, and ever-elusive goals — that some people find racing hard to resist. Some runners also find that racing offers a childlike appeal that calls us back to some playground in our distant past when some kid said, "Hey, race you to the monkey bars and back to the steps!"

Of course, the toughest races are always the ones we run against ourselves. According to John "the Penguin" Bingham, who pens a beginner's column in *Runner's World* magazine, racing is a good way to outrun your own personal demons — be they past, present, or future. A former trombone player who once loved to party, Bingham didn't begin running until age 43, when he became disgusted with his overall physical condition and outlook on life. He began by waddling through his runs at a pace slower than 10 minutes a mile, but he now completes dozens of races a year, including marathons. To echo the words of the Penguin's proud racing credo: "The miracle isn't that I finished. . . . The miracle is that I had the courage to start."

Think Small — At First

You can nourish your dreams of racing by taking a gradual, low-key approach. Or to put it another way, don't make your racing debut in the New York City Marathon, with 20,000-plus runners and 26.2 miles staring you in the face.

Instead, look for a local 5-K run (3.1 miles) on a flat course. Shoot for a time of the year when the odds of reasonable running weather — moderate temperatures and low humidity — are in your favor. Recruit a training partner of similar ability and mind-set to run the race with you to share both support and the experience.

Some newspapers list upcoming races in the sports section, but for lists of races all around the country (or even international events), check running magazines such as *Runner's World* and *Running Times*. In this age of Web browsing, you can also track down races online.

Sometimes you can find a 2-mile fun run that accompanies a longer, more serious race, such as a 10-K. The 2-mile fun run is a good break-in race for novices, especially people who are apprehensive about their racing debut.

Runners with a cause

If you aren't all that keen about racing for yourself, consider doing it for someone else. Charity races — such as Race for the Cure, which benefits breast cancer research, or Team in Training, which is helping fight leukemia — gathered great support in the 1990s and have raised millions of dollars. People who would never consider themselves tough or competitive are often astounded to find what reserves they can muster when they're out there running for those less fortunate than themselves.

Before a Race

Good racing inevitably can be traced back to consistent training. If a runner is poorly trained, then the best race strategy and the lightest racing flats in the world will be of little help.

But if you've done the work, then you simply need to stay calm and relaxed in the days just before the race and on race day. Being prepared and relatively organized can help reduce your anxiety levels, too.

The night before

Get your racing gear — warm-ups, racing shoes, socks, shorts, and singlet — laid out the night before. If you've already picked up the packet with your race number, then pin it to your racing singlet so that you won't have to worry about it in the morning. (Some races, particularly big ones, have packet pick-up the day before the race. This packet includes your race souvenir T-shirt and perhaps other freebies, such as a water bottle, key chain, or headband.) Double-check the weather report to see whether your clothing requirements might change by the time the morning rolls around.

When pinning your race number to your singlet, be careful not to pin the rip-off bottom finisher's tag! Race officials tear this off after the runners finish to tabulate the results.

Start hydrating more than normal several days before the event. You may not want to drink a whole lot in the morning hours just before the race.

The morning of the race

Breakfast is always an individual call. Some runners can wolf down a short stack of pancakes three hours before they go to the line, while others prefer only half a plain bagel washed down with a few ounces of a sports drink. Experiment on the morning of your training runs so that you know what your body needs — and can handle — in terms of food and fluids.

If the race is short and fast, such as a 5-K, go to the starting line feeling light, not full. But if it's a long race, like a marathon, you don't want to feel hungry after only 10 miles of running.

Getting there

Give yourself more time than you think you'll need to drive to the race. Even some Olympic athletes have been known to miss their events because they've been stuck in heavy traffic en route to the stadium. Allow for the unexpected delay, and your nerves will be better for it. It's better to be a little early and have extra time for the warm-up, stretching, and a last visit to the bathroom.

Tour the course

If you have time to spare, check out the course map and locate any key features, such as a major hill, a bridge to be crossed, aid stations, or a tricky turn. Even if you are not expecting to be up with the lead runners, knowing what's coming is always a help. You might even do your warm-up on part of the course, especially if you can jog over the final mile of the route (easy to do on a "loop" course that starts and finishes in the same spot); that way you may recognize some landmarks on the course as you near the end of the race.

If you have time, jog out from the finish line (opposite of the way the race will finish) to check out the last half-mile of the course. Pick out a landmark, such as a church, a road sign, or a tree, and plan to pick up the pace from that point on during the race.

Dress for success

When in doubt, go to the line dressed in clothing that you can use — or get rid of. For example, if it's a 40-degree day and you can't decide whether you need racing gloves or not, wear them! You can always chuck them late in the race if you get too warm, or you can tuck them in the elastic band of your shorts. You can do the same with a pullover ski hat on a borderline day in March.

During the Race

At the start, be honest and line up with the group shooting for finishing times that are within your reach. At big races, signs that read 6-minutes-per-mile pace, 7-minutes-per-mile pace, and so on designate where runners should start.

Pay attention as race time approaches. When the gun goes off, you may not be able to run right away because the participants are packed together so tightly. Shuffle along with your hands up — or lightly on the back of the runner shuffling in front of you — until the field strings out and you have room to run. Try to avoid weaving in and out in the first half-mile. In addition to increasing chances of "runner pileup," weaving often wastes energy that may come in handy late in the race.

In a very crowded race, swing wide on the early turns on the course. You'll run a bit longer, but you'll avoid the crush of bodies on the inside turn and keep a steady, consistent pace.

Race the conditions

Skiers talk about "skiing the conditions." If they encounter an icy slope or a blinding snowstorm, they make adjustments in their racing strategies. Runners, too, must consider the weather. If you arrive on race day morning and are greeted by 30-mile-per-hour headwinds or temperatures rising toward 90 degrees, then make allowances in your time goal.

Hot weather (see Chapter 10) in particular demands that you use your brain early in the race. Start at a conservative pace and drink plenty of water early and often. In a hot race, especially a half-marathon or marathon, you'll need water about every 15 minutes.

Think positive!

Running is a big mental game in addition to the physical challenges. But even if your race isn't unfolding exactly how you hoped — you're running slower than your time goal, or you aren't feeling comfortable — focus on finishing.

Count down the miles in a race to reinforce to yourself that you are making progress to the finish. But when the going gets tough, sometimes the next mile mark or aid station seems like a long way off. A good mental trick is to key in on something closer, like the next street, the fire station up the block, or even the next telephone pole — whatever you need to keep on truckin'.

The pack attack

Even if you are attempting to finish ahead of as many of your fellow runners as possible (and usually that applies to experienced racers in the top 10 percent of the field), working in cooperation with others also makes sense.

A pack of five or six runners cruising through the miles together tends to feed on group energy. On a breezy day, runners in a pack can take turns breaking the wind, an overall energy-saver for everyone in the group. Runners in a group also share water or energy gels, too. After all, the clock and the distance are the real adversaries!

Keeping the inner demons at bay

Just as some runners are naturally somewhat nervous at the start of a race, some runners have doubts during the race, particularly during what British runners are fond of calling "bad patches."

When you hit a bad patch, try to focus on something other than your discomfort, such as proper running form. Try to stay relaxed and coax yourself through it with positive self-talk. Tell yourself, "I can get up this hill" or "I can get through this."

Energy gels can provide a late race lift, especially in a half-marathon or marathon. Most energy gels provide between 70 and 100 calories per pack. They're light to carry (especially tucked inside racing gloves) and a good carbohydrate reload on the run. Try the gels in practice first (the same with sports drinks) before using them on race day.

The Finish

If you feel relatively good in the final mile, try to build into a strong finish. Don't wait until you actually see the finish line banner to make your move. Go sooner. If you are simply flying toward the finish, then probably you saved too much for the end. Make a mental note to spread your effort out more evenly in the next race.

After you finish, take care of any potential problems, such as blisters. Always rehydrate, even if you don't feel thirsty. Eat within an hour of finishing a race because your muscles will be most receptive to replenishing fuel. In cold weather, seek out warm, dry clothes or shelter.

Some races offer snack foods — bananas, yogurt, energy bars, cookies — at the finish. Eat something to hold you over, but try to eat a larger meal in the following two hours to refuel your body.

Some races offer free post-race massage. A light rubdown can soothe tired muscles. But if you suspect that you have a real injury, opt for RICE — Rest, Ice, Compression, and Elevation (covered in Chapter 15).

If all this sounds like common sense, understand that you are not always thinking clearly at the end of a race, especially a marathon. Of course, some people may argue that anybody who enters a marathon wasn't thinking all that clearly to begin with!

Cool Your Jets

Unless your workouts have been extremely promising for a novice runner, or you have a deep (and relatively recent) background in a sport that requires a lot of endurance (like soccer, lacrosse, serious cycling, or long-distance swimming), don't line up near the front. Be content to start in the middle of the pack or, if you are unsure, even at the back of the pack.

Because even a low-key race is likely to have your adrenaline pumping overtime, resist the temptation to sprint off the first minute of the race. Instead, settle into a comfortable pace, perhaps just a tad faster than a typical training run. You should be breathing comfortably enough that you could ask your training partner a question — or answer a question.

It's perfectly natural to be a tad nervous in the last hour before a race. To neutralize the effect of pre-race nerves, focus instead on your warm-up routine. After the starting gun goes off, race day nerves usually disappear in short order.

Through the middle miles of a race, concentrate on your pace. Check your mile splits on your watch or the race clocks at each mile marker. Also remember to monitor how much energy you feel you have left to cover the rest of the distance. Keep in mind that your body can usually do more than you might think possible in the middle of a race! Think positive!

Splits is just a runner's term for the amount of time it takes to run a certain distance. For example, if you ran the second mile of a 5-K race in 8 minutes, then 8 minutes is your split for that segment of the race. A miler on the track typically talks about his lap splits; usually one for each quarter-mile, or one lap of the oval.

When you get close to the end of the race, perhaps with 3 or 4 minutes left until the finish line, try to pick up the pace. If you started out conservatively and paced yourself, you may be surprised by what you can do now. Don't wait until the last 10 seconds, when you see the finish line banner, to come steaming in; try to start increasing the speed before that and spread your energy out over the last half-mile or so of the course.

If you are struggling, then simply slow down and keep moving. (Veteran marathoners refer to this as "the survivor's shuffle.") Even if you need a short walk break or two, there's glory in persevering. The last mile of a tough race can seem like an eternity, but you'll get there.

Beware the Racing Bug

The time just after you run your first race — especially if you found your virgin voyage to be an exhilarating experience — can hide some potential pitfalls. Here are a few dangers to watch for:

- **The training maniac:** This runner returns to training and suddenly goes bonkers, jumping up from 20 miles per week to 40 or 50, thinking, "If I train harder, I'll race much faster next time out." But a rapid rise in training volume or training intensity can greatly increase your injury risk. With that in mind, increases in both mileage and quality sessions should be very gradual. The 20- or 30-mile-a-week runner should add no more than 3 to 5 miles per week at a time.

- **The racing bug:** This runner likes the racing experience so much that he or she signs up for a race every weekend for the next three months. But if you over-race, then you run a risk of injury or simply becoming stale — in essence, too much of a good thing.

- **Marathon fever:** Some runners finish their first 5-K, and two months later — without any other race experience — they've entered their first marathon. A much saner, safer approach is to run five or six shorter races over the course of a full year. Some of the races should be in the 10-K (6.2-miles) and the half-marathon (13.1-miles) range. And, of course, would-be marathoners need to increase their weekly long runs in training before tackling the 26.2-mile beast.

The patient plan

After your initial fun run debut, don't race for at least a month. Go back to training, with perhaps a gradual increase in mileage and effort as you begin to get in shape. Wait until you have some breakthrough training runs, the kind that make you think, "Wow. That was a lot easier than the last time I tried it" after you're done. Then it's time to think about trying another race.

Some coaches offer this analogy to their runners: Training, both the miles and the quality days, is like putting money in the bank. Racing, because it takes a lot of effort, is like taking money out of the bank. Returning to training after a few races makes sense. It's a way to build up your bank account again.

Goal!

Goals aren't just for World Cup Soccer. Pick a modest, doable goal for your next race. (But having a dream goal on the back burner of your brain is a good idea, too.) For example, perhaps you ran 28 minutes (or about 9 minutes per mile) in your first 5-K, and that pace felt relatively comfortable. You finished, recovered quickly, and maybe even thought, "I can run faster than that!" A doable goal might be 27:30 in your next 5-K. If you go a bit faster than your goal, all the better.

Even pacing is your best bet when setting time goals. Your pace may vary due to the terrain because uphill miles are understandably slower than flat miles. An evenly paced effort, however, will get you to the finish in good speed and in relative comfort.

Go into every race with a plan. The plan may be something as simple as "I'm going to stay with Joe for at least the first 2 miles and then see how I feel" or "I'll start comfortably and then see how I feel once I get over the big hill at the halfway mark." But do have some idea of how you want to approach the race.

Chapter 14
Marathon or Bust

A mystique surrounds the marathon, a 26.2-mile race that some people view as an exotic journey that only a few runners can take.

"If you want to run, run a mile," said Emil Zatopek, the great Czech Olympian of the 1950s. "If you want to experience another life, run a marathon."

Talk like that scares the running shorts off many beginners. It shouldn't. The truth is, you don't have to be a masochist or a macho man or woman to run a marathon. Any healthy individual can do it — provided that you've got the will and the way. We show you the way in this chapter, but a little extra motivation never hurts anyone.

Marathon Experience Gets Rave Reviews

The reviews are in! Here are some quotes from runners about their marathon adventure:

✔ "Crossing the finish line was probably the most extraordinary experience of my life, next to childbirth. I was high from it for months."

✔ "You're probably not going to win the race, but you will be a winner with your family and friends. Because when you've done a marathon, you've done something a lot of people wish they could do."

✔ "Running the marathon gave me an inner strength that changed my life."

- ✔ "I felt that if I could do this, I could do almost anything."

- ✔ "The marathon is my benchmark. It is the status symbol in my community, the running community."

- ✔ "The marathon is charismatic. It has everything. It has drama. It has competition. It has camaraderie. It has heroism. Every jogger can't dream of being an Olympic champion, but he can dream of finishing a marathon."

Those last two quotes are especially important because they were spoken not by average runners but by two of the most influential members of the running community.

The late Dr. George Sheehan, who spoke about the marathon as "the status symbol in my community," inspired thousands of people to take the marathon challenge, in his books, articles, and lectures. A sort of running philosopher, Dr. Sheehan said that running was a natural part of our lives and that through the marathon people can learn a lot about themselves.

The late Fred Lebow called the marathon "charismatic," an adjective that also describes Lebow. Lebow was a visionary and a wonderful promoter. As the cofounder and director of the New York City Marathon, the goateed Lebow, a middle-of-the-pack runner, helped expand the marathon from an event that only Olympians and kooks could do into a mass movement, a spectacle, and a happening. The New York City Marathon eventually became the world's largest marathon — 31,456 runners finished the NYC Marathon in 1998 — and an event that has become an annual tradition and practically a holiday in the Big Apple.

The origin of the word "marathon"

The word "marathon" is used in many contexts, most having little to do with running. The U.S. Congress holds marathon sessions when a controversial bill is on the line. Your local home electronic stores have marathon sales. Cable TV presents *Brady Bunch* marathons. So, although *marathon* has come to mean almost anything of great length, the word does have a specific meaning — and a specific distance. The word gets its name from the Plains of Marathon in Greece, where, legend has it, the first marathon was run by a long-distance Greek courier named Phidippides. The official distance of the modern marathon, whether it's the Boston Marathon, the New York City Marathon, or the Athens Marathon, is 26.2 miles.

A Marathon Program for the Long Run

The lure of the marathon can be powerful. Before you go charging out of the gate, remember that you need a little time and seasoning first. Beginning runners should wait six months to a year before moving up to marathon training. This period gives your body the time to adapt to running. Gradually working up to a marathon gives you the chance to adapt to your new running lifestyle, making the kind of healthy changes that will help build a foundation when you're ready to take on the ultimate challenge.

You can choose from many proven marathon training programs, but the one we like best was developed by Jeff Galloway, a 1972 Olympian who has successfully coached thousands of first-time marathoners.

Galloway's runners go the distance because the program is simple, conservative, and designed to get you to the starting line in one piece. It's based on just three days of running per week (plus cross-training), which gives your body plenty of time to rest and recuperate from the most grueling and important component of marathon training: the long run.

Which race should I do?

Before you begin to plan your marathon training, you need a marathon to train for. More experienced runners, those looking to run a good time in a race, often choose smaller races because they're concerned about getting across the start line quickly. Other runners look for races with flat courses or few turns.

As a first-timer, you shouldn't worry about the number of participants or the race course. You're in it for the experience and the sense of achievement. A mega-race can enhance that sense of adventure. It's also an opportunity to visit a new city or to see a familiar city from a new perspective.

So choose your marathon and then begin working backwards. You need four months to prepare. Also keep in mind that most marathons are held in the fall or spring. Cooler weather is generally better for a marathon because you're burning 2,000 to 3,000 calories and generating plenty of body heat over the course of 26.2 miles.

The outline of a simple training program

How do you prepare for a marathon? The training philosophy is easy really, no matter whose program you follow. You start at whatever distance you can currently run, and gradually build up your mileage until you've reached the point where you can cover 20 or more miles in your training.

The beginning program that we outline here is very simple. From Monday through Saturday, you do basically the same thing. You run a little and cross-train a lot. These activities put less wear and tear on your joints and keep you fresh and motivated about your running.

The only thing that changes in this program is the Sunday long run, which gets longer and longer.

Here's a schedule of what your typical week of training should look like:

Sunday: Long run

Monday: Rest

Tuesday: Weights or cross-training

Wednesday: Run from 30 to 45 minutes

Thursday: Weights or cross-training

Friday: Run from 30 to 45 minutes

Saturday: Walk or cross-training

Build up your marathon training mileage by following this schedule for your weekly long runs:

Week	Miles
1	6
2	8
3	10
4	6
5	12 to 13
6	6
7	15 to 16
8	7

Week	Miles
9	18 to 19
10	8
11	20 to 22
12	10
13	10
14	22 to 24
15	8 to 10
16	8 to 10
17	The marathon (26.2)

You can alternate the long runs with faster-paced runs or workouts in hilly areas, if you like.

The long run

The long run teaches your body how to burn carbohydrates and fat efficiently and how to deal with the mental and physical strains of running for long periods of time.

Now a word about time: Don't worry about it in your long runs. You should focus on just getting through, finishing the distance, and feeling good about your achievement. The second time around, if you want, you can shoot for a time goal.

Walk and run

Don't worry about going *fast* during your long marathon training runs. Your challenge is to go *long*. That means you should run slowly, maybe a minute slower than your normal training pace. Galloway also recommends walking breaks — a minute of walking for every 3 to 5 minutes of running.

How long?

Gradually increase the length of your long runs, adding 1 to 3 miles every other week until you're near marathon distance. Just how near is one of the controversies of marathon preparation. Galloway advises runners to actually go the distance (26.2 miles) in training. Other coaches recommend no farther than 20, or even 18, miles. We come down in the middle — literally. We recommend that you do 23 to 24 miles for your last long run, which should be done three weeks before the race. That way, your body is accustomed to a run of near-marathon distance, yet you still have a goal to achieve on race day.

Making it through the long runs

There's no way around it. If you want to run a marathon, you've got to do the long runs. Here are some tips on how to survive these long runs and — dare we say it? — maybe even make them enjoyable!

- ✔ **Start early in the day.** Do your long run on Saturday or Sunday morning. Most people have jobs, families, and responsibilities, even on weekends. An early start allows the runner to still have a good part of the day after the run for other activities. A morning run also keeps you from training in the hottest part of the day.

- ✔ **Make sure that you plan a route with access to water.** Maybe you can map out a route that passes by a water fountain in a local park. Or you may have to run loops that pass by your car or home several times so that you can grab water each time.

- ✔ **Restock your energy supplies.** Doing a 20-miler on an empty stomach is not a great idea. The advent of energy bars and gels has made it easier for endurance athletes to get the calories they need. But, of course, you can also munch on a banana or a bagel when you get up. Because everyone has different food requirements during exercise, experiment to see what works best for you during a long run. Then take that knowledge with you into the race. You might try a bar or a gel packet before your run, and then another halfway through.

- ✔ **Seek out the company of friends and training partners.** In marathon training, running companions become more essential than ever. Why? Because you're going to eventually get to the point where your long runs will keep you out on the roads for 2 or even 3 hours. That's a long time! Make it pleasant and stimulating by running with others.

- ✔ **Look at the long runs not as punishment or an ordeal but as a challenge** in and of themselves. They can be rewarding, fulfilling, and even fun. Above all, they are essential to your marathon preparation.

Life besides the long run

What should you be doing on the six days of the week that you're not doing a long run? Well, you'll probably find that you won't want to do much of anything the day after your long run. In fact, you'll probably need a little more sleep and sustenance in general during a marathon program.

The whole idea of this program is to maximize your endurance while mini-mizing your chances of injury. Beginners who get really gung-ho about marathoning are usually cruisin' for a bruisin'. They launch into the long runs with gusto and insist on running again the next day, and the next, and the next. Although you may be able to get by with five or six days of running a week in general, those doing their first marathon build-up should not be running that much. Those longs runs can be fun, but they take a lot out of you. For that reason, we suggest that you keep your other two or three runs during the week relatively short. If you want to throw in some hills or a little fast running, fine, but don't do it on the day before or after your long run.

The other days of the week, we urge you to cross-train. For a more complete picture on cross-training for running, see Chapters 16 and 17. Activities like weight training, swimming, and cycling provide benefits to your body while giving your feet a break!

Three weeks and counting

A friend of ours was planning to run his first marathon. But the pressure of his job kept him from training properly. He tried to play catch-up. A few days before the race, against our pleas, he went out and ran 20 miles — the longest run of his program. He was so sore the next day that he could barely get out of bed. On race day, he forced himself through 12 miles before he had to drop out. This training mistake marked the end of his training program and the end of his marathon dream. Last we heard, it was the end of his running altogether.

You should do your last long run — about 23 miles — three weeks before the race. That will give your body plenty of time to recover. Also, you may want to wear a new pair of shoes at that point. (Make sure that you first break them in during a couple of your shorter runs during the week.) If you've been training in the same pair for all your long runs, you're probably due. And breaking in a new pair on race day is not a good idea.

You've done your last long run? Congratulations. The tendency for many beginners at this point is to want to do more, to fine-tune, and to get in yet another long run. Resist that urge. Studies show that it takes about 10 days for the benefits of cardiovascular training to take effect, so beyond that point, nothing you can do really is going to help you improve, anyway.

And take a lesson from our friend. Don't try to play catch up. If things happen in your life that prevent you from completing your marathon training, fine. Drop back to your regular level of running while you come up with a new plan and a new race to shoot for. Remember, there's always another marathon, but there's only one *first* marathon.

Eating for the big race

There is no such thing as a good marathon diet. There is something called a good, wholesome diet that all runners — indeed, all healthy people — should follow. That diet includes plenty of fruits, vegetables, and grains; some protein; and, yes, some fat, as well. You should follow the same quality diet during your marathon program. As far as quantity, your body will be your guide. And it will probably tell you — a little more frequently and a little more forcefully than it normally does — that it's hungry. Don't skimp on the food, but be careful what you feed it. A marathon program is not a green light for ingesting mass quantities of junk food.

We can't stress enough the importance of a balanced diet. Pasta, for example, is certainly one of the best sources for complex carbohydrates. So bon appétit! But as you shovel down that forkful of rigatoni or angel hair, remember that pasta, bagels, rice, and other carbohydrate-rich foods do not a diet make — even a diet for marathoners.

The week before the race

What should you do the week before the race? Whatever you've been doing all along. That's right. Now is not the time to make changes in your eating or sleeping habits.

Try to get one or two days of complete rest leading up to the race. The day before, you may want to stretch your legs, probably by walking a little bit. And there's nothing wrong with a very easy jog of a mile or two, if only to help soothe the nerves.

Use that time to mentally take care of the little details, from deciding what you'll wear on race day to planning how you'll get to the start.

Many races have pasta parties the night before the race. Some runners stuff themselves like Thanksgiving turkeys. Don't follow in their tracks. Eat well, but don't gorge yourself.

On race day, make sure that you're tanked up and ready to go: Again, don't experiment with new foods or bars or gels. Rely on what you learned from your long runs. But do eat something. Running on an empty stomach is a mistake that many beginning marathon runners make. They pay for it at mile 22 or so when, all of a sudden, their fuel gauge hits "E."

Things to do 24 to 48 hours before the marathon

Nothing can replace the months of training you've done for your first marathon. You can't go out and fake 26 miles. But you can do some things in the days leading up to the race that can affect just how well and how comfortably you'll run on the big day:

- ✔ Get a good night's sleep on the two nights before the race. Research shows that this is when sleep counts most. Don't forget to set a back-up alarm or get a wake-up call from your hotel on race morning.

- ✔ Make sure that you know how you're getting to the start of the race and how you're getting home from the finish. If you're uncertain of locations, consult your race kit or call the race office.

- ✔ Plan what you're going to wear based on current weather conditions. Don't overdress: A singlet and shorts are sufficient for all but the coldest marathon conditions. Make sure that they're clothes you have run in before. To keep comfortable while you're waiting around at the start, plan to bring an old, long-sleeve T-shirt or sweatshirt and a pair of gloves that you can discard after the race starts and you're warmed up.

- ✔ Pin your number to your race shirt the night before. (Why start the morning of the marathon by drawing blood — especially your own?)

- ✔ Clip your toenails.

- ✔ Pack a bag that will be waiting for you at the baggage check area at the finish. Include a bottle of water, an energy bar or a piece of fruit, some emergency money, and a change of clothes for after the race.

- ✔ Drink plenty of water before the race.

- ✔ Try to get off your feet a little bit. Visit the race expo, for example, but don't spend all day there.

- ✔ Relax as much as you can. Read a good book or watch a movie on TV. The less tense you are going into the race, the better you'll run.

- ✔ Walk over to the staging area of the race so that you know where you're going the next morning. You may even want to walk or drive the last mile or so of the course so that you'll know on race day when the end is near.

Running the Race of Your Life

The start line of a major marathon is an exciting place to be. Balloons are released, rock music is playing, and announcements are blaring over the public address system. Crowds of spectators have gathered, and hundreds, maybe thousands, of runners are buzzing with anticipation.

It's easy to get caught up in this atmosphere and to allow yourself to go out too fast. Remember what you're there for: to finish and feel good about it. You'll see lots of "hot dogs" go speeding by you. Don't follow them. Chances are, you'll see them again later, when their initial enthusiasm is tempered by the reality of 26.2 miles.

Instead, focus on staying relaxed and in rhythm. And make sure that you stop and take fluids at every water stop, even if you don't feel thirsty. Many marathons now have food and gel stops, as well. If you've tried these during your long runs, fine. If not, pass them by.

When you hit that first mile, don't think "Okay, only 25.2 to go." Instead, break the race up into segments: 5-K, 5 miles, 10-K, 10 miles, half-marathon, 15 miles, 20 miles, 25, 26.2. At each of those checkpoints, think about how far you've come and how good you feel. Don't worry about how fast you're going. You should feel very comfortable for the first half of the race.

Remember that most successful marathons are run as *negative splits,* meaning that the second half is faster than the first. Even though your goal in your debut marathon is not a fast time, you should strive for the same approach, which requires careful pacing and keeping plenty in reserve. When in doubt, slow down, especially in the first 20 miles of the race.

Runners often say that a marathon begins at the 20-mile marker. No matter how well you've trained, the last 6.2 miles will probably be challenging. Now is the time to dig deep and to think about those long runs and the training and effort you've put into it. Focus on good, smooth running form.

Hang tough. The finish line's in sight. At last! You've done it! When you cross the line, smile for the camera and keep walking.

Yes, we said camera. Most major marathons take a picture of every finisher. (Plus, you can be sure that friends and family will have their cameras and VCRs on hand as well.) The race photographer will send you a proof in the mail a few weeks after the race, and you can then buy as many glossy photos of yourself as you want.

After the Race

Savor the moment and then get your baggage, change into some warm-ups, and keep taking fluids. A hot bath, a dip in a pool, some stretching, or a massage later will ease the soreness. So will 20 to 30 minutes of walking. Yes, one of the best things you can do after a marathon is walk — even if it's later that day. And don't run for the next week or so. Walking, cycling, and swimming are fine, but give your body a break from the pounding.

One last tip for race day. Have fun that night! You've earned it. You're a marathoner.

Part IV
Fine-Tuning

The 5th Wave   By Rich Tennant

©RICHTENNANT

HAPPY BIRTHDAY, CATHY

"Okay, look—I know you wanted a treadmill for your birthday, but I came up with an even better idea..."

In this part . . .

*B*ecoming a great runner involves training in activities other than running. We provide advice on both cross-training and strength training. We also help you to deal with injuries, and to top things off, we offer some additional words of wisdom for women, kids, and seniors who run.

Chapter 15
Injuries and How to Treat Them

• •

In This Chapter

▶ Reducing your risk of injury

▶ Treating common injuries

▶ Finding out what ailments plague runners

▶ Searching for specialized help

▶ Performing the walk test

• •

An injured runner visited a sports podiatrist and was told that his pain was caused by some biomechanical problems in his running gait. The podiatrist recommended orthotics — special corrective shoe inserts designed to combat his faulty biomechanics — and sent him on his way.

Six months later, the runner was back again — injured again.

"I thought you said I'd never get hurt again if I got orthotics," said the runner.

"I never said that," said the podiatrist.

"Well, how come I think you said that?" said the runner.

"Because you're a runner," said the podiatrist. "And most runners are crazy."

Runners aren't *really* crazy, but when it comes to injuries, especially if it means taking some time off from running, we aren't always the most patient of people. We want to be better and back running, if not yesterday, then at least by tomorrow.

Injury Avoidance Strategies

Of course, the best way to deal with running-related injuries is to avoid as many of them as possible in the first place. But completing an entire running career over two or three decades without a injury that knocks you out of training for a week or two is akin to walking across a minefield with a blindfold and making it to the other side. It's been done, but it takes the kind of luck that belongs in a Las Vegas casino.

Nevertheless, you'll greatly reduce your odds for injury if you follow this advice:

- ✔ Stay well hydrated. Muscles in a well-hydrated body will be less prone to cramping or straining.

- ✔ After you've logged 300 to 500 miles in a pair of running shoes, buy new ones. Remember, shoes are cheaper than doctor visits!

- ✔ Don't run in super-light racing shoes (under 7 ounces) that offer minimal support, especially if you land heavy. Consider light trainers (9 or 10 ounces) as a more supportive alternative.

- ✔ Don't run in your basketball or tennis sneakers and don't play hoops or smash backhands in your running shoes!

- ✔ Run as much as you can on forgiving surfaces, such as cinder and dirt paths or closely cropped, flat grass.

- ✔ Avoid running on roads that are *crowned* (or *cambered*); the uneven surface can bring on aches and pains.

- ✔ The beach is a good place to read a book or jump a wave, but it's a bad place to run. Running on the slope toward the ocean can kick up various aches and pains. If you can't resist, find the flattest stretch possible and switch directions every 5 minutes.

- ✔ Be aware that a sudden switch to a surface that you aren't used to — such as loose sand, snow, ice, or a rain-slick road — can sabotage your usual running gait. When your natural running style is altered, you stand an increased risk of injury.

- ✔ Complement your running with a flexibility and strength-building program.

- ✔ Don't try and train through the subtle, little injuries. If you ignore a small injury, it will likely get worse.

- ✔ Always warm up and cool down. These easy jaunts before and after a workout can help reduce lactic acid levels in the body and keep your legs loose for tomorrow's run.

Lactic acid build-up is the waste by-product of a hard working muscle. The accumulation of lactate in the blood is what makes you feel sore after a killer workout, especially if you suddenly increase the intensity or length of your sessions. But endurance training helps your body flush lactic acid from the blood with greater proficiency.

✔ When mapping out your yearly training program, factor in some downtime. Runners need some periods of reduced training, cross-training, or even complete rest from running.

Train, don't strain

Few pearls of wisdom in sports can outshine the advice to "train, don't strain." But runners are usually better at recommending such advice to other runners than practicing the advice themselves. Runners are more likely to treat the much-uttered phrase like a traffic light changing to yellow — the advice serves more like an optional caution.

Recognize the signs of overtraining (see Chapter 12) and take some time to rest and recover. Overly tired runners are prime candidates for a running-related injury.

Too much, too soon

Sports medicine professionals familiar with running-related injuries believe that runners get hurt because they do too much, too soon.

Rapid increases in mileage — or intensity of workouts — can place a runner in the danger zone. That's why sports medicine professionals refer to the vast majority of running injuries as "overuse injuries."

The good news is that most running injuries affect the soft tissue, meaning that the injuries are strains, as opposed to broken bones, and heal rapidly with some simple treatment and rest.

Great Ways to Treat Injuries

Before we discuss the various and sundry injuries, we mention a couple treatment methods that are commonly used on most of the injuries that you may, heaven forbid, encounter.

RICE is nice!

Among the running set, RICE is the key word for dealing with injury. Here's what that acronym stands for:

- **R is for Rest:** Take time off! No dedicated runner likes downtime, but attempting to grit your teeth and train through a slight injury can, at best, hinder the natural healing process. At worst, the slight injury can become more serious and knock you out of running for weeks or even months.

- **I is for Ice:** At the first twinge or hint of an injury, slap an ice pack on the hot spot. Just 15 or 20 minutes of the cold treatment will reduce inflammation. (Don't keep the ice on much longer than 20 minutes in one spot because you can cause freezer burn to your skin.)

- **C is for Compression:** For best results, wrap the ice pack right to your leg if it's a hamstring or quadriceps muscle. Compression helps reduce swelling.

- **E is for Elevate:** If possible, raise the injured area above your heart. Flop on the couch, an ice pack wrapped to the injured muscle, and prop the leg up on a couple of pillows.

If you don't have an ice pack, try freezing some water in a small paper cup with a Popsicle-type stick. After it's frozen solid, remove the ice from the cup and, using the pop stick as a handle, give your wounded area an ice massage for 15 to 20 minutes. A bag of frozen peas, wrapped tightly around a sore muscle, also works.

RICE is a good first counterattack choice for runners. It's easy and cheap. But if after 48 to 72 hours of RICE (don't cheat on the Rest part!) the injury isn't responding (or seems worse), then seek professional medical advice.

Some runners reluctantly give in and take one day off for a slight injury, but you really need two or three days of rest for even the little nagging stuff (a sore calf muscle or a tight hamstring, for example) to simmer down.

Anti-inflammatories

In addition to RICE, anti-inflammatory drugs, such as aspirin or ibuprofen, can help reduce pain and soreness. But follow recommended dose guidelines to the letter; you don't want to completely mask low-level pain and inadvertently do more damage to the injured area. Pain is your body's warning defense system, so shutting that system off is not wise.

Don't fall into the trap of using anti-inflammatory drugs as a crutch simply so that you can get your workout "fix" in for the day. If over a period of several weeks you are still using anti-inflammatories so that you can train, then chances are good that you really need to take time off or visit a sports medicine professional, or both.

Large doses of anti-inflammatory drugs (especially when used beyond the recommended amount) can increase the effects of dehydration. Runners who exceed recommended amounts, particularly in long races (such as a marathon) on hot days, can even risk kidney failure.

Common Running Injuries

Five of the most common running injuries are shinsplints, chondromalacia (also known as runner's knee), Achilles tendinitis, plantar fasciitis, and iliotibial band (ITB) syndrome. Stress fractures, which usually occur in small bones in the foot, leg or shin, also show up in runners who overtrain. In addition, runners must constantly guard against blisters, strains, and other problems that can hinder their efforts.

Shinsplints

Shinsplints are a common complaint among beginning runners. Shinsplints usually involve a tenderness in the soft tissue areas on the front-inside of the lower leg. The injury throbs and feels sore but sometimes loosens up as exercise progresses.

Rookie runners suffer from shinsplints simply because their legs aren't used to the stress of running. But running in worn-down shoes, or in shoes made for other fitness activities, can also play a role, as can your choice of running surfaces.

How to treat

RICE is your first line of counterattack. But an immediate decrease in training is usually required before shinsplints will simmer down. Head for the pool or the exercise bike for some non-weight-bearing exercise.

When you come back to running

Continue to cross-train, and gradually begin to add some light running. Stay off hard surfaces, especially concrete! Steer clear of steep downhills to cut down on pounding. Avoid overstriding, because landing hard on your heel (with a virtually straight leg) will radiate shock right up your leg.

Shinsplints are sometimes mistaken for a much more potentially serious injury called *compartment syndrome* (a swelling of the muscle in the compartments of the lower leg). In extreme cases, the swelling muscle can feel rock-hard. If your shin pain persists or you feel a swelling sensation in the shin area, make sure that a sports medicine professional rules out the possibility of compartment syndrome.

Chondromalacia, or runner's knee

When it comes to the percentage of running injuries, knees lead the pack of pain. *Runner's knee* has sort of become a catch-all label for any kind of knee pain that runners come up with, just as any kind of shin pain is, rightly or wrongly, often lumped together in the shinsplint category. But sports medicine professionals know runner's knee by its scientific name of *chondromalacia.*

Runner's knee flares up when the cartilage under the kneecap takes on a sandpaper texture because of constant grinding against other cartilage. Inflammation around the edges of the kneecap is common. As if the pain isn't enough, this injury sometimes makes a racket, too — snap, crackle, and pop sounds can occur during movement.

How to treat

RICE and moderate anti-inflammatory drug use can help alleviate the symptoms. In some cases, sport orthotics can help because overpronation in the running motion can be a cause. You can also try building up the quadricep muscles (by adding straight leg raisers with light weights to your strength program) because strong quads can combat movement of the kneecap (patella). A patella that doesn't "track" properly usually results in knee inflammation.

When you come back to running

For a few weeks, avoid running on hills with steep descents and steer clear of crowned roads. Continue to work on quad-strengthening exercises, even after the pain is gone. Ice down any lingering hot spots around the kneecap.

Achilles tendinitis

The Achilles tendon is a potential trouble spot for most runners. When the Achilles tendon is forced to endure an inordinate amount of work, such as excessive speedwork or killer hill sessions, then this fibrous tendon can inflame, and the pushing-off motion of foot-strike can turn painful.

Who was Achilles?

Achilles was the most fleet-of-foot of all the Greek warriors to attack Troy, but the hero was vulnerable in the tendon just above the heel. That's because (according to legend) his mother held him by the heel when she dipped him into the mythical river Styx in an attempt to make her son immortal. As fate would have it, Achilles later took an arrow in that one unprotected spot.

An Achilles tendon can also rupture or partially rupture. Although rare in long-distance runners, a torn Achilles tendon is a serious injury and requires expert medical attention and, in most cases, surgery.

How to treat

RICE and anti-inflammatory drugs can help relieve the pain of Achilles tendinitis. Don't try and stretch an already painful tendon; you could make the injury worse. Instead, opt for cross-training to maintain your fitness. For an Achilles injury, consider running in a swimming pool because you'll avoid pounding. If you ride an exercise bike, be careful not to push the toughest gears (those gears that give lots of resistance); be content to spin briskly in the lighter gears.

When you come back to running

Add some light calf stretching and toe-raisers to your warm-up after your Achilles tendon is completely pain-free. Here's a simple calf/Achilles stretch: Put your hands on a wall, with your body at an angle. Carefully exercise your calf/Achilles area by lifting a heel slightly up (with your toe still touching the ground) and then gently pushing the heel to the ground, using a smooth, controlled motion. Start with just 5 to 10 reps (don't do the exercise to the point of discomfort) and then gradually add more reps in future sessions. In the early stages of your comeback, avoid hills and hard speedwork.

Plantar fasciitis

The plantar fascia is a thick fibrous band of tissue in the bottom of the foot that runs from the base of the toes to the heel. When the plantar fascia becomes overly tight, or is overly stressed, then a runner can develop pain and inflammation, usually under the arch of the foot. This condition is known as plantar fasciitis. Runners with flat, rigid feet — or runners who insist on running in worn-out shoes — are prime candidates for plantar fasciitis.

Because the plantar fascia tends to gradually loosen up with use throughout the day, those first barefoot steps in the morning are often the most painful. Runners with plantar fascia problems should slip right into shoes before they hit the floor, so that the area does not get immediately — and severely — stressed.

How to treat

In addition to RICE, some runners find relief in a couple of easy-to-do home remedies.

Towel trick

Sit barefoot in a chair and toss a towel on the floor in front of you. Then reach out with your toes, gripping the towel, and pull it toward you. Repeat the process for 10 to 20 times daily (or twice a day if you find the time) while you're watching TV. The gripping motion of the toes will gradually stretch the plantar fascia and help it become more flexible.

Golf game

Some runners find relief from plantar fascia soreness by rolling a golf ball back and forth under the arch of the foot. This exercise massages the trouble spot. You can also try gripping the golf ball with your toes, as in the towel exercise.

Orthotics

Orthotics, special shoe inserts usually made from a cast of the runner's foot, can help some flat-footed runners fight plantar fascia woes. The devices lend arch support and can cut down on pronation.

When you come back to running

Continue to treat yourself, even after you think you're cured. Ice the plantar fascia for 15 to 20 minutes immediately after a run. Pay special attention to wear and tear on your running shoes. In extreme cases, consider wearing your orthotics in your everyday shoes for added support and motion control throughout the day.

Iliotibial band syndrome

Iliotibial band syndrome (also known as ITB syndrome) just sounds like it must be bad news for runners!

The iliotibial (IT) band is a large ligament that runs along the outside of the leg between the hip and the knee. More often than not, a runner feels soreness on the outside of the knee as the first signs of ITB syndrome, but it can also strike where the ligament attaches at the hip. Sometimes the entire band can just feel extremely tight. Runners with bowed legs or runners who overpronate (that is, their feet roll in too far upon striking the ground) are prime candidates for ITB problems. Runners who have one leg longer than the other can also suffer from ITB syndrome.

Because the ITB often heats up from the frictionlike rubbing at the knee (or hip), runners may start a run feeling okay, only to have the afflicted areas feel sore and inflamed along the way.

How to treat

You can't train through ITB problems, so drastically reduce the duration of your runs or stop running completely. And the RICE treatment also helps.

One of the most effective (and simple) stretches is to stand with your right leg crossed behind your left, and your left arm against a chair, table, or wall. Shift your weight against the object as you push your right hip in the opposite direction. Keep your right foot firmly on the floor while allowing your left knee to flex slightly. This gently stretches your ITB down the outside of your right thigh.

When you come back to running

Continue to make an ITB stretch part of your warm-up routine. Avoid downhill running, tight tracks, or crowned roads. Find running shoes with good motion control or consider orthotics if a sports podiatrist recommends them.

Beyond the Big 5: Other injury woes

The next batch of injuries ranges from the common to the uncommon and from the serious to the not-so-serious.

Stress fractures

Stress fractures — micro-cracks in the bones of the feet, legs, or occasionally even the hip or pelvic areas — can knock a runner out for as much as six weeks or more. Stress fractures are typical of an overuse injury. Military doctors termed them "march fractures" because raw recruits forced to trudge off on long marches would sometimes incur the tiny breaks.

The fractures may first appear to be nothing more than a nagging ache, but the pain will build if you attempt to keep training. Even an x-ray doesn't always reveal whether you have a stress fracture. When a thin white line does appear on an x-ray, the fracture may already be in the healing process.

Good horse sense

Thoroughbred race horses get stress fractures, too. And if the Kentucky Derby is coming up on the schedule, then their trainers don't want the horses getting out of shape. So they put the horses in the pool and make them swim in deep water to maintain fitness. Water exercise works for humans, too, because running in water provides a challenging cardiovascular session and works several muscle groups — all without impact to the injured limb.

One method that sports medicine professionals use to more accurately determine a stress fracture is a bone scan, but the relatively expensive test involves putting a radioactive dye into the body. Elite athletes in a big hurry to return to competition might opt for a bone scan, but the average fitness runner should probably pass on it unless your doctor deems it absolutely necessary.

Here's an early warning sign of a possible stress fracture: an achy sensation that occurs when you press on one particular spot with a finger.

Strains

Runners are occasionally sidelined with a strained hamstring (the big muscle in the upper back leg, below the buttocks) or calf muscle. RICE is the way to treat mild strains, but if the injury feels extremely painful and unresponsive to first-line treatments, then check in with sports medicine professionals.

A chronic area of injury, such as the hamstrings, needs stretching and strengthening as good injury-prevention measures. For example, leg curls can strengthen weak hamstrings. Deep tissue massage can also help speed recovery from most common strains.

A good weight room or fitness center most likely has a leg curl machine. Lie flat on your stomach on the exercise bench, lifting light weights toward your buttocks in a slow, steady effort. If you need to jerk the weight up, or are unable to do at least 8 to 10 repetitions without getting tired, then the weight is probably too heavy. Get an instructor to supervise your initial lifts.

Sciatica

When the sciatic nerve gets irritated, it can be — literally — a real pain in the rear for runners. Pain can radiate from the buttocks and down the back of the leg. Sciatica is sometimes mistaken for a hamstring injury. In some cases, the pain may feel like you've been abruptly zapped with an electric current. Sciatica can sometimes kick in when you're sitting.

Runners with tight hamstrings or runners who have one leg longer than the other are especially likely to feel the sting of sciatica. Use anti-inflammatories and pay extra attention to stretching, particularly the hamstrings and the muscles of the lower back. Monitor sciatica carefully, and if you can't shake it with self-treatment or by cutting back on running, then seek out the sports medicine professionals before it gets worse.

Side stitch or side "sticker"

A side stitch isn't technically an injury, but this nagging ache does cause runners to slow down or stop. Side stitches are usually caused by a cramp in the diaphragm or too much food in the stomach. A sharp painful or cramping sensation, usually under the rib cage, a stitch almost always pops up in the middle of a hard workout or race. If you stop running, the stitch typically goes away within minutes, but it can come right back if you start running fast again.

Side stitches seem to occur more often if you eat too close to workout time or even if you chug down a quart of fluid right before you start a run. (For this reason, it's best to drink water throughout the day and then just drink a moderate amount in the 30 minutes prior to a workout.)

How do you get rid of this pain in the side without actually stopping your run? Try changing your arm position: Raise your arms straight up, with your hands above your head, for a few minutes as you slow to a jog, or let your arms hang straight down by your side. Some runners, but not all, can find relief from a stitch with these tricks. Otherwise, try slowing to a jog for several minutes and then gradually speeding up again.

Blisters

Blisters are small problems that can become big problems if they lead to infection. Almost every runner suffers from blisters at one time or another, but they should be treated seriously.

Here's how to treat them:

1. **Clean the area around the blister, preferably with iodine alcohol or another solution with the ability to kill germs.**
2. **Sterilize a needle in boiling water.**
3. **Pop the blister with the needle and push gently on the blister (with clean gauze) to drain the liquid inside.**

    This step should ease the discomfort.

4. **Apply salves or ointments that protect against infection.**
5. **Cover the blister with a clean adhesive bandage, such as a Band-Aid or Second Skin.**

If you suspect that the blister is infected (it throbs painfully and appears red and swollen), then seek professional medical attention immediately.

Ankle sprains

Ankle sprains are one of the few running injuries that aren't usually the result of overuse. Ankle sprains happen suddenly: A runner stumbles over a rock, trips on a tree root, or steps off a sidewalk the wrong way.

Don't try to run off (or even walk off) a turned ankle that's even slightly painful. Instead, try to get ice on the ankle as soon as possible and elevate your leg. Check for swelling and discoloring; if you notice these symptoms, then seek medical attention to assess the extent of damage.

Runners who have chronic ankle sprains should try to run on flat, smooth surfaces. Sometimes the ligaments of an ankle that's already suffered previous sprains will be relatively loose, thereby increasing the risk of another sprain down the road.

Heading for Help

Experienced runners tend to seek help from doctors, health care professionals, or therapists who have experience treating other runners. You should, too. Some running clubs have sports medicine specialists among their members. You can also ask coaches in your area where they send their injured athletes for treatment.

Runners don't usually visit their family doctor with their latest injury. But a generalist is a good choice when runners get sick. If you have signs of a cold, the flu, or respiratory problems, consult your family doctor before you continue training, especially if you have a fever.

Podiatrists

Runners with foot or ankle injuries often seek the advice of a podiatrist, someone specially trained to treat foot problems. Runners may also turn to podiatrists for some relief from above-the-ankle injuries that may originate in the foot. For example, some hip or knee pain can result from biochemical faults or slight structural flaws that may be affected by the continual foot strikes of runners.

A sports podiatrist who understands the mechanics of running can often help runners compensate for those faults. Typically, that means fitting the injured runner with orthotics. Custom-made orthotics, molded to your foot, usually run in the $200 to $300 range, but many formerly injured runners swear that they're worth every penny.

When you visit a podiatrist, take your old running shoes with you. A foot doctor can sometimes determine your biomechanical problems by examining the wear patterns on the bottom of your shoe.

To find a sports podiatrist in your area, contact the American Academy of Podiatric Sports Medicine at 301-424-7440.

Massage therapists

Massage can rub many runners the right way. A massage not only helps maintain flexible muscles but also relaxes runners, makes them happier, and can improve their performance. Even a weekly, half-hour sports massage can help speed recovery to sore hamstrings, calves, or tight quadriceps. Expect to spend $20 to $30 for a half-hour massage.

Physical therapists

Physical therapists can be the answer if you're looking at a long recovery, such as weeks or months, from a bad injury. Physical therapists sometimes have access to treatments such as ultrasound that you won't have in your home remedy arsenal.

Ultrasound is used to bombard a deep tissue injury with high-frequency sound waves. The vibration effect of the sound waves is believed to increase blood flow and speed the healing process.

A top-notch sports medicine clinic, staffed by both doctors and physical therapists, can offer the latest in rehabilitation equipment, too. The downside is that physical therapy can be expensive (sometimes $80 an hour or more) unless your health plan picks up the bulk of the tab.

To locate a physical therapist in your area, call the American Physical Therapy Association at 800-285-7787.

Chiropractors

Certified chiropractic sports physicians specialize in physical manipulation and spinal adjustment treatments for various injuries. To consult with a chiropractor in your area, contact the American Chiropractic Association Sports Council at 800-593-3222.

Orthopedists

Most running injuries, especially the overuse variety, heal with rest and traditional treatments. But if traditional treatments and lots of rest don't help you get back on your feet, then it may be time to call in the heavy artillery. If you have severe muscle tears or other traumatic injuries to muscle, bone, ligament, or nerves, you should probably see an orthopedist, a physician who specializes in skeletal deformities. Some orthopedists focus on a specific part of the body, such as the knee.

Surgery should almost always be a last resort for a runner. Try all the nonsurgical methods of rehabilitation first. Before you decide to have any serious operation, get opinions from other doctors.

Call the American Orthopedic Society for Sports Medicine at 708-803-8700 to consult with an orthopedist in your area.

Comeback Kids

Very few running injuries are career-ending. You can increase your chances of a successful comeback by following the recommended treatment advice and by not rushing your return to running.

The length of time that you spent on the sidelines and the treatment and exercises you used while you were recuperating can make a difference in the time it takes to get back in shape. If you did some cross-training and were diligent about your rehabilitation extras — such as stretching, icing, and strengthening weak muscle groups — then your return to running may be quicker than you think. But don't rush it!

Shinsplints, tendinitis, and strains have kept me on the sidelines a few times in my career — but never for too long. To cut down on injury risk, I lift weights, stretch, and get massage therapy.

The Walk Test

Just as the talk test is an excellent guideline for those beginning to train, the walk test is a good method to gauge whether you're ready to resume training after an injury.

Don't even *think* about running again until you are walking 100 percent pain-free, including treks up and down flights of stairs. When you can walk a few miles pain-free, then you might start adding several minutes of light jogging interlaced with walking stints. These initial jogging and walking sessions should not last more than 2 or 3 minutes to start. If you have pain while jogging, then return to walking for a few days before you try jogging again later. If you have no pain while jogging, then you can begin to add on some minutes to your training — gradually!

Choose a flat cinder path or an all-weather track (with some "give" to its surface) and try something like this: 5 minutes of brisk walking, 2 minutes of jogging, 3 minutes of walking, 3 minutes of jogging, 3 minutes of walking, 2 minutes of jogging, 5 minutes of brisk walking.

No doubt you'll feel pumped to be back out there, but resist the urge to run every day. Instead, go every other day for at least a week or two, gradually reducing your walk breaks and increasing your running until you can jog 15 to 20 minutes pain-free.

Don't set a deadline for your return to running, such as "I'm going to jog on Monday, no matter what." Let your body determine when you are ready to return to trotting.

As you re-enter the running world, avoid hills until you begin to see real fitness gains on the flats. After you pile up days of pain-free running, increase the length of your runs and then gradually weave some light quality workouts back into your training schedule. A return to racing should come only after you can run some moderately intense quality workouts without any sign of pain from your old injury.

Chapter 16

Cross-Training and Treadmill Training

In This Chapter

▶ Safe cross-training

▶ Good cross-training exercises

▶ Cross-training equipment

▶ Treadmill training

*I*f you keep on running long enough, you'll find out why we devote a chapter to other forms of training. If you keep on running hard enough, you'll see why runners are also cyclists, swimmers, and walkers. And if you keep on running frequently enough, you'll see why an entire new sport — the swim/bike/run event called the triathlon — has emerged from the ranks of rundown runners.

Running too long, too hard, or too often leads to overuse injuries, muscle imbalances, and pure staleness. To prevent these problems, today's runners are generally more multi-faceted in their fitness activities than their predecessors, who basically ran, ran, ran, and eventually ran into trouble. Over time, even the fastest and most talented of athletes learn the lessons of cross-training.

FLO-JO SAYS

Before I suffered an injury, I believed in only running. I loved other sports, but I couldn't see myself doing anything else while I was training hard in my own sport. But when I got a bad case of shinsplints, I had no choice. The pain was so excruciating — physically and mentally — that I had to start doing other activities to stay fit. And you know what? Eventually, I began to enjoy these other activities. Injuries made me a cross-training believer.

Don't wait until you get hurt to learn the same lesson. Both novice and veteran runners can start now to practice the healthy habits that will keep them on the road for years to come. And one of those healthy habits is cross-training.

Is cross-training just an advertising slogan or perhaps a way to sell more shoes? Maybe to an extent cross-training serves those purposes. But the concept behind the commercials is sound. Basically, cross-training means participating in fitness activities other than your primary sport. Cross-training for runners can include walking, swimming, deep-water running, cycling (on both a stationary and outdoor bike), cross-country skiing, and virtually every other form of exercise available in a health club.

In this chapter, we discuss these major forms of cross-training to help you find one or more that suits you. We also include treadmills in this chapter. Although technically treadmills are not a form of cross-training but another way to run, treadmill running gives you a break from the pavement and provides a change of pace. (The one form of cross-training that we don't discuss here is weight training. You can find that information in Chapter 17.)

Cross-Training: How Much? How Often? How Hard?

Pedaling a stationary bike won't make you a better runner. To improve as a runner, you have to run. Makes sense, right? But running all the time is probably going to leave you hurt, tired, or burnt-out. If you add cycling or any other form of cross-training to your exercise routine, you can maintain aerobic fitness while giving your body a break.

We recommend that you run no more than four to five days a week. On the days that you don't run, you should probably try and incorporate some weight training and, if you like, some aerobic cross-training. (Also, don't be afraid to take one day off completely! It's a cliché but still valid: The most overlooked aspect of many training programs is rest.)

Coaches and exercise physiologists also talk about training cycles — that is, dividing the year into several different cycles or periods, based around your competitive schedule, and adjusting your training accordingly. You may or may not be racing yet. But this principle of *periodization* can still apply to you, even though you don't have to use that fancy term. After all, you don't need a Ph.D. in exercise physiology to recognize the best times of year to run: The dead of winter and the dog days of summer are not those times. During those times, you may want to incorporate a little more cross-training in your training regimen.

And, of course, if you do suffer an injury from running, cross-training becomes vital. You don't want to lose that hard-earned fitness. You don't want to see the weight come back. You don't want to go stir-crazy from inactivity. Cross-training is the answer.

Cross Safely

What do running, rowing, racewalking, riding a bike, swimming and cross-country skiing all have in common? They are all forms of cardiovascular or aerobic exercise — the kind of exercise that works your heart and lungs. And so the basic training principles for all these activities are similar.

The duration of your cross-training exercise sessions should be from about 20 to 60 minutes (closer to 20 to 30 minutes when you're first starting out), plus a warm-up and cool-down. Your intensity level can be calculated in many ways: You can wear a heart monitor and have it set to your training zone. You can estimate (roughly estimate) that training zone by subtracting your age from 220. Exercising at between 50 percent and 70 percent of that number should be about your training zone. For example, a 40-year-old man or woman, who is starting an exercise program, wants his or her exercising heart rate to be between 90 and 126 beats per minute.

Two other, easier ways to gauge exercise intensity are the talk test (which we talk about in Chapter 4) and rate of perceived exertion (RPE).

RPE is an abbreviation for a fancy term for a simple idea. RPE stands for *rate of perceived exertion* and means that you gauge your own intensity on a simple rating scale. "Perceived exertion," says Thomas Scandalis, D.O., associate professor of sports medicine at New York College of Osteopathic Medicine in Old Westbury, New York, "may be the single best way for an individual who doesn't want to go through testing or relying on mathematical formulas or heart monitors to get into their target training zone."

Although we're discussing RPE here in the context of other cross-training activities, you can use it for your running, too. The scale, called the Borg Scale after its inventor, is based on a ranking of 6 to 20. Any effort under 6 requires the presence of a recliner, a TV set, and a big bag of potato chips. Anything close to 20 means an all-out, gut-busting effort.

Moderate-hard exercise — the aerobic zone where you want to be — has a value of 13 to 14. (Beginners should stick to 10 to 12.) Although this scale is obviously subjective, an exertion rate of 13 or 14 should mean that you're working hard, feeling a little out of breath (but not a lot), and able to speak only in short sentences.

The Best Cross-Training Exercises for Runners

Exercise physiologist Owen Anderson, Ph.D., editor of *Running Research News,* ranked alternative forms of training for runners. What exercise appeared at the top of his list? Weight training. We agree that weight training is important, so it merits its own chapter (17) in this book. Here are the other top cross-training exercises, in order:

- ✔ **Cycling:** Several studies have shown that cycling can help improve running performance. In one study, runners who trained on stationary bikes improved their 10-K race times by 9 percent. "I was surprised at the effectiveness of cycling for runners," Anderson said. "I knew it provided a good cardiovascular workout, but I didn't realize it was specific enough to help runners improve performances."

- ✔ **Soccer:** Surprising? Not when you consider that during a typical game, players cover between 9,000 and 11,000 meters, including 4,000 meters of jogging, 2,000 meters of running at high speeds, and between 800 and 1,000 meters of outright sprinting. "A soccer competition is like an excellent, prolonged interval workout," says Anderson. Here's the proof we need: Many of the top Kenyan runners were originally fine soccer players.

- ✔ **Deep-water running:** Anderson ranked this activity number four, behind cycling, weight training, and soccer, citing tedium as one of the drawbacks. (Accessibility to a pool is another disadvantage.) Other exercise experts are more bullish on the value of deep-water running, also known as aquajogging. In this exercise, you run in deep water while tethered to the side of a pool, or you run back and forth in a designated lane while wearing a flotation belt or vest.

  Stan James of Eugene, Oregon, one of the top orthopedic surgeons in the country for runners, thinks that deep-water running is the single best form of cross-training for runners because it allows them to continue to run without any of the impact force of running on a solid surface.

- ✔ **Stair climbing:** Anderson believes that by improving the aerobic capacities of your quadriceps, this activity will "transform you into a hill-climbing demon." He cites a recent study in which individuals who participated only in stair-climbing workouts for nine weeks improved their running performances as much as athletes who engaged in regular running sessions.

The rest of the list includes, in order, cross-country skiing, aerobic dance, walking, racquet sports, swimming, and, at the bottom, golf, which Anderson wryly observes, "is only slightly better than cigar smoking."

Keep in mind that Anderson was looking at how these activities specifically helped running performance. All of them — well, all right, maybe not golf — help you maintain fitness and give you a break from running. The key is to choose one that's right for you.

Choosing Cross-Training Equipment That's Right for You

What's the best kind of exercise equipment on the market?

That's one of the most commonly asked questions by people who want to get in shape and by runners recovering from injuries or those who want to incorporate cross-training into their regimens, in order to avoid injuries.

That was the same question posed by a group of researchers from the Medical College of Wisconsin in Milwaukee. In a major study published in the *Journal of the American Medical Association (JAMA)* in 1996, the researchers compared subjects' perceptions of which machines provided the best workouts. The researchers based those evaluations on the RPE — which we explain in the "Cross Safely" section.

Here are some of the pros and cons about the common types of cardiovascular exercise equipment used in the *JAMA* study, how much they cost (if you're looking to buy), plus an indication of how much energy you expend while using them.

Cross-country ski simulators

Cost: $200 to $700

Calories burned per hour: At 5 to 8 mph, 610

Advantages: Cross-country skiing is one of the best indoor workouts money can buy. Cross-country ski machines use both upper and lower body muscles, thereby burning more calories. Also, unlike running, you're not putting any strain on your joints. It's a smooth but challenging workout.

Disadvantages: Can you walk and chew gum at the same time? If not, you may not have the patience to learn how to use this machine. Unlike some other forms of equipment, you can't just hop on and go.

Stationary bicycles

Cost: For the standard, upright bike (the kind used in the *JAMA* study), expect to pay from $200 to $500. If you want bells, whistles, and computerized hill programs, the cost can go up to $2,500.

Calories burned per hour: At 13 mph, 545

Advantages: A stationary bicycle is for you if you're on a budget, you don't have space for a treadmill, or you're just starting out on a cross-training program. Stationary bikes are stable and they're familiar. Plus, it's easy to watch TV or read while you pedal away.

Disadvantages: Some folks find bikes boring. They'd rather be on their feet.

Dual-action bikes

Cost: The Schwinn Air Dyne, the model used in the study, costs about $600. Other dual-action models are in the same range.

Calories burned per hour: At a vigorous pace, approximately 600

Advantages: The fact that the handlebars move along with the pedals makes this a better workout than the standard stationary bike because you're using your upper body, too. Also, the open flywheel design keeps cool air coming your way during the whole workout.

Disadvantages: Many women find the seat uncomfortable. So if you're considering a dual-action bike (or any other stationary bike, for that matter), make sure that the seat is comfy enough for the long haul.

Rowing machines

Cost: $700 for the Concept II, the model used in the study; $200 to $1,500 for other models

Calories burned per hour: At a vigorous pace, 815

Advantages: Rowing is a tough, challenging exercise that works your trunk muscles, something that most machines don't do.

Disadvantages: The rower is not a very popular machine in most gyms because it takes time to learn the proper technique.

Stair steppers

Cost: $200 to $500 for the manual types; $600 to $2,000 for the electronic models

Calories burned per hour: 410

Advantages: Stair steppers provide a good workout and a familiar workout, especially for those who have spent any time in health clubs, where stair steppers and treadmills are the two most popular forms of exercise equipment.

Disadvantages: The stepping motion aggravates some people's knees. And because runners tend to have knee problems, you may want to be careful with this kind of equipment. Also, make sure that you perform the exercise correctly. To properly use a stair stepper, stand erect and get the full range of motion in both legs.

Exercise riders and elliptical exercisers

The *JAMA* study didn't include some of the new forms of indoor training apparatus: exercise riders and elliptical machines. As with all kinds of exercise equipment, some people swear by them. But in the case of the riders, just as many people are swearing *at* them. In its January, 1997 exercise equipment guide, *Consumer Reports* offered this evaluation: "Never before has exercise equipment we tested performed as poorly as the riders." The magazine conceded that, although they may be good for beginners, "there are better ways to get in shape."

We know one better way to get in shape: running. And in lieu of that, we know others: the other cross-training activities we list in this chapter. That doesn't mean you can't get a decent workout on a rider. So be careful if you choose one, and, as with all of these forms of indoor exercise equipment, make sure that you try them out first. Get a day pass at a local health club and experiment with the different forms of equipment. Then make a decision.

While you're at the club, you're sure to see the hottest new type of cardio-vascular equipment — elliptical exercisers. On these machines, you stand on two platforms, which are connected to a flywheel, and move each leg in an elliptical or oval-shaped motion, without any of the jarring impact of running. It's a smooth, comfortable, and effective motion when you get the hang of it. However, *Consumer Reports* also found that the home models had big problems.

The best advice for now is to use the elliptical models found at your local health club, which is a good option to consider for cross-training in general.

A health club offers a range of equipment, access to weights and personal trainers, plus classes — such as indoor cycling — that can complement your running program. You may also want to use a club as the start and finish point for your runs. In addition to shower and locker facilities, you also may find training partners among the other members.

Treadmill Training

Although all the various cross-training exercises had value, a 1996 *JAMA* study found that the exercise equipment that was perceived as being the best, burning the most calories, and forcing subjects to work the hardest was the motorized treadmill. (Non-motorized treadmills are not recommended for runners.)

In my opinion, nothing beats a treadmill workout when you don't want to run outside. A good movie, some water, and a little ventilation are all you need.

Here's why the treadmill is an excellent way for runners to get or stay in shape:

- ✔ It has a more forgiving surface than your sidewalk, which helps minimize the impact force to your body. (Today's tread surfaces, in fact, can absorb up to 40 percent more impact than outdoor surfaces.)
- ✔ It's a safe, controlled environment.
- ✔ It offers you a way to keep running comfortably, no matter what the weather.

But treadmills do have some drawbacks:

- ✔ Treadmills are expensive.
- ✔ Running on treadmills can be mind-numbingly boring.
- ✔ Although treadmills can provide a good workout, running on them is not quite the same workout as running outdoors at an equivalent speed.

Of course, there's nothing wrong with a slightly less demanding run. In fact, sometimes, it may be just what the doctor ordered. But if you want to make sure that your treadmill run is a workout that's roughly equivalent to your outdoor run, set the incline at 1 percent instead of running on a level plane. This adjustment compensates for the lack of air resistance or wind that you battle against when you run outside.

Treadmills are king

According to the Fitness Products Council, consumers spent more money on treadmills than on any other major piece of equipment — about $1.5 billion in 1997. In that same year, an estimated 36.1 million Americans exercised on a treadmill at least once, according to the Sporting Goods Manufacturers Association, an increase of about 32 million from 1987. And at health clubs, the lines form at the treadmills: The number of people using these machines at gyms has climbed from 1.1 million in 1987 to 7.4 million in 1996, according to the International Health, Racquet, and Sportsclubs Association.

Some people run almost exclusively on treadmills. Some clubs even hold treadmill marathons. Sometimes, especially in winter, people in northern climates training for spring marathons are forced to do their long runs on treadmills. Having done several 20-milers on a treadmill, we don't recommend it as a standard practice. Nor do we recommend doing all your training on a treadmill. But it can be done, and the treadmill has undoubtedly become a valuable tool for runners.

Tips on buying treadmills

If you want a treadmill for your home that you can run on for years to come, you're going to have to shell out at least $2,000.

It's money well spent, say the experts. "The better the machine, the more comfortable the machine, as well," says Richard Miller, owner of the Gym Source in Manhattan. "The less jarring and rattling, the more time you're likely to spend on it."

After you've decided to make that investment, keep in mind that, although the electronic bells and whistles — the calorie counter, the computerized hill profiles, the built-in heart monitor — are all nice features, they're not nearly as important as the overall construction. A good general rule on which to base your decision is the weight of the machine: Generally, the heavier, the better.

Look for a machine that has a net weight of 200 pounds or more. And while you're looking, give it a workout. "Jump around on it and see if you hear noises and squeaks," says Miller. "The less noise you hear, the better."

Here are some other considerations when shopping for a treadmill:

- ✓ **The belt:** This is the surface that your feet touch. Most treadmill belts are two layers thick; some have extra layers of rubber for more shock absorption.

- ✓ **The length:** Most treadmills are 45 to 60 inches in length. If you have a long stride, go for a longer treadmill.

- ✓ **The width:** A treadmill that's at least 18 inches wide gives you enough room; any narrower and you may feel like you're walking through a crowded subway car.

- ✓ **The shut-off switches:** Most treadmills have emergency shut-off switches. But some are located on the console of the machine in places that are all too easy to accidentally hit while you're running.

- ✓ **The reliable names:** In treadmills, the ones to look for include Trotter, True, Landice, Precor, and Aerobics/Pacemaster.

- ✓ **The comfort and ease of use:** Test-run on your treadmill. Play with the elevation and the speed. See how it responds, how it feels, and whether the controls are easily accessible or not.

Some treadmills also come with heart monitors, calories counters, and computer consoles that allow you to program hill routines and all kinds of workouts. Some day soon, you'll probably be able to go online or watch TV on a built-in treadmill console. All of these things are fine extras, but remember, they are just that: extras. The power, durability, and quality of the treadmill should be the most important factors in your purchasing decision.

Top home treadmills for runners

Runner's World magazine ranked the single best home treadmills for runners. Here were the models and their suggested retail prices:

- ✓ Landice 8700 Series: $2,395 to $4,295

- ✓ Life Fitness Life Stride 5500HR: $3,495

- ✓ PaceMaster Pro-Plus: $1,795

- ✓ Precor 945: $4,195

- ✓ Trotter 510: $3,695

- ✓ True Fitness 450HRC: $2,795

If these prices are making you feel faint but you still want a treadmill at home, keep in mind that you can often find good buys on these and other models in the secondhand market. Check the classified ads in your local newspaper. Some cities even have sporting goods retailers who specialize in secondhand fitness equipment.

How to use treadmills

Because treadmill running is a little different from running on the roads, you may need some time to get used to it. Many people feel that they need a couple of sessions before they get their "sea legs," so don't immediately start clicking off the miles as soon as you hit the start button.

Start your treadmill running program the same way you started your outdoor running program: walking. In this case, the idea is to get used to having a moving surface under your feet.

Try to walk without hanging on to the console or gripping the side rails. After you feel comfortable — after a couple of sessions — then you can start running. You may feel as if you need to shorten your stride or compromise your form a little bit to conform to the dimensions of the treadmill, and to some extent, you probably will. But, as with running form in general, eventually your body will probably fall into the most efficient stride for you (see Figure 16-1).

Figure 16-1:
After a few sessions on a treadmill, you'll develop a comfortable stride.

The placement of your treadmill is also important. Folks who have tread-mills in their bedrooms tend to end up using them as clothes hangers. It's probably a better idea to put your treadmill in a designated place, such as a basement or a recreation room, that's as far away as possible from the distractions of everyday life, most notably the refrigerator. Try to locate your treadmill near a window. You'll especially enjoy the view if you're running on your treadmill while the wind is howling and the snow is blowing outside. On days like that, you'll feel sorry for those who have to run outside, but you'll feel all warm and fuzzy about the wisdom of your tread-mill purchase.

To beat treadmill boredom, distract yourself by watching television or a movie on your VCR. Most health clubs have TVs set up in front of their treadmills. If you're using a treadmill at home, consider setting up a TV and a VCR in front of it. Or put your boombox nearby and run to the rhythm of your favorite music or radio station.

Although we strongly urge you not to run with headsets when running outdoors, you can listen to music while you run indoors, and do it safely. Music can make the miles go easier. Studies have shown that people who exercise to music have a lower rate of perceived exertion, a topic that's discussed in the "Cross Safely" section earlier in this chapter. They felt better and more relaxed, probably because the music, like movies, dis-tracted them from their efforts.

In addition to music or a TV and VCR, you may want to have a full-length mirror in front of you so that you can monitor your form as you run. Having a fan or a source of cool or fresh air is wise, especially when you start working up a sweat on those long runs.

Although some people talk on portable or cell phones while they run on their treadmill, we don't recommend it. It's hard to run while holding a phone in one hand. Besides, part of the point of running is to get away from that kind of interruption for a little while.

What to watch on your treadmill

Here are the authors' choices for what to watch and what to avoid while running on a treadmill:

John's best bets for treadmill TV:

- ✔ *Patton:* Long, loud, and inspirational.

- ✔ *The Longest Day:* Ditto.

- ✔ Any PBS documentary on a subject that interests you: No commercials.

- ✔ Ken Burns's PBS *Civil War* series: Ennobling and involving. And with nine episodes, you could stretch it out to last almost as long as the war itself.

- ✔ Televised races and marathons: We know somebody who overslept for the New York City Marathon one year and instead ran the entire 26.2 miles on his treadmill while watching the TV broadcast of the race.

Flo's best bets for treadmill TV:

- ✔ *It's A Wonderful Life:* Flo's all-time favorite.

- ✔ *The Wizard of Oz:* Something uplifting as you follow your own Yellow Brick Road.

- ✔ Documentaries on inspirational athletes: My heroes include Jesse Owens, Wilma Rudolph, Sugar Ray Robinson, and my own sister-in-law, Jackie Joyner-Kersee.

Save it for the couch:

- ✔ Network programs: They have too many commercials, and using a remote to fast-forward or channel surf while you're running is too hard!

- ✔ Evening news or talk shows: The former are too depressing, and the latter are too static.

- ✔ Late night reruns: Who wants to watch that many dating service commercials?

- ✔ Infomercials: They'll try and convince you that you bought the wrong piece of equipment. Don't listen to them.

Chapter 17
Strength Training

. . . .

In This Chapter
▶ How strength training can improve your running
▶ Why weights won't make you too muscular
▶ Which exercises to perform

. . . .

*I*f you had picked up a book on running 10 or 20 years ago, you wouldn't have found a chapter like this. Strength training? Why, that activity wasn't for runners. That was for big, hulking guys who covered their bodies in oil and grunted as they tried to strike bizarre poses. But you don't want to look like a bodybuilder, do you? And, as long as you have endurance and speed, who needs muscles anyway?

The answer is, you do. Runners don't necessarily need the same kind of strength that a bodybuilder, a football player, or a sprinter needs. But runners do need enough strength to help keep their upper bodies erect in the waning hours of a long run or a marathon, enough strength to help their legs absorb the impact force of running, and enough strength to lift themselves out of a tub or up the stairs when they're in their 70s and 80s!

What Lifting Can Do for Your Running

Susan Kalish, executive director of the American Running and Fitness Association in Bethesda, Maryland, is unequivocal on the subject of weight training. "Runners come to me and ask, 'What can I do to improve?'" says Kalish. "I'd say if you're going to do one other thing besides running, it's strength training. There is proof that a good strength training program will reduce your rate of injury, and there is proof that strength training will make you faster."

Exercise physiologist Owen Anderson, Ph.D., concurs. In his ranking of the best cross-training activities for runners — the activities that most directly help running performance — weight training is Number 1 on the list.

The value of strength training

Among the top runners, Steve Spence of Chambersburg, Pennsylvania, provided perhaps the most dramatic testimonial to the value of strength training. In 1991, when Spence couldn't even run because of injuries and illness, he hired a strength coach and began an aggressive weight training program. Four months later, he won the bronze medal in the marathon at the World Championships in Japan. It's still considered one of the best performances by an American distance runner in this decade. Since then, many other top American runners — including Alberto Salazar and Ann Marie Lauck — have made weights a part of their programs, with excellent results.

Why?

As numerous studies over the past decade have shown, weight training has been found to improve the way you run. It can help correct muscle imbalances and, above all, prevent injuries.

The most common of these imbalances among runners is in the legs: Runners typically have really strong hamstrings and really weak quadriceps. That can lead to knee injuries. A strength training program that includes the quads can reduce the risk of these problems. Many elite distance runners now incorporate some form of resistance work into their regimens to help prevent such injuries.

What Lifting Can Do for the Rest of Your Life

Top athletes aren't the only ones who benefit from strength training. The American College of Sports Medicine and the U.S. Surgeon General's office have both made twice-weekly weight training sessions a part of their exercise guidelines for all Americans — with good reason. Strength training has been shown to be a major preventive measure against osteoporosis. In addition, a series of now-famous studies done in nursing homes found that a regular regimen of strength training enabled even patients in their 90s to stop using their wheelchairs and start walking on their own. After some of these patients stopped the weight training, however, they returned to the wheelchairs.

So the message about your muscles is clear: Give 'em a lift — with strength training.

Training, training, training

Weight training. Strength training. Resistance training. All of these terms are used almost interchangeably. Basically, these terms all mean the same thing: Your muscles are working against a force (resistance) that taxes them to the point that the muscles must literally grow to "meet" this resistance.

As long as I run, I will always lift weights. To me, running without weight training is like running barefoot because something so valuable is missing. I don't lift weights now as heavily as when I was a sprinter — and needed that explosive power out of the blocks — but I still lift consistently, three or four times a week. I try to work all the muscle groups — upper and lower body — because I know that if I want my body to continue to take me places, it's got to be strong!

"Weight training will make me tight and inflexible." Baloney. That common belief has been proven to be false in running and most other sports. No study has shown decreased range of motion (flexibility) among people who train with weights. In fact, some studies have shown just the opposite.

Many objects can supply the resistance in resistance training. Physical therapists use plastic tubing, and aerobic instructors use weighted batons. Some folks use soup cans, unabridged dictionaries, or other weighty objects around the house. You can even use your own body weight, by doing push-ups, for example.

Pump and run

A few years ago, Wayne Westcott, Ph.D., strength consultant for the YMCA, developed a weight lifting program for the girls' cross-country team at Notre Dame High School in Hingham, Massachusetts. His program emphasized all the major muscle groups, not just the muscles used in running. He was careful to make sure that the girls performed their exercises correctly and consistently. The results?

Over the four-year period, Notre Dame high won four consecutive girls' state cross-country championships. During that time, only one athlete suffered a running-related injury — an incredible record. "These strength-trained runners were able to withstand demanding workouts without breaking down," said Westcott.

To keep you from breaking down, pick up a weight.

But the most effective form of resistance comes from free weights (dumbbells and barbells) or the kind of weight training machines found in most health clubs. These weights can be raised or lowered easily; they offer a wide variety of movements for the various muscle groups; and you can safely and comfortably perform exercises with these weights.

Arnold, You're Not My Type (The Difference between Runners and Lifters)

Runners are different from most of the folks who head into the gym. Runners want to run. They want to spend less time in the weight room and more time on the roads. Their goal is also different from many people — particularly men — who join the local health club. Runners don't want to get big. Oh sure, a little muscle definition under the race singlet wouldn't be bad. But runners don't want anything that's going to make us trade in our running shorts for posing trunks.

If becoming too muscular is your concern, don't worry. Most people — men, as well as women — don't have the testosterone levels, or the muscle type, to accommodate that kind of big muscular growth. Most runners tend to have a higher percentage of Type I muscle fibers — the so-called "slow twitch" endurance fibers — than your average fullback or powerlifter, whose muscles have more Type II muscle fibers — the "fast twitch" type that they need for explosive power.

Research by Wayne Westcott, Ph.D., a strength consultant for the YMCA, has shown that Type I muscle fibers respond better to what is known in strength circles as a "high reps, low weights" approach. "NFL players get better results with heavier weights and fewer repetitions," says Westcott. "Runners need to train with higher repetitions because they have a great energy reserve system. To get the same level of fatigue, you have to go longer. And to go longer, you need a little less weight."

High *reps* (short for repetitions) doesn't mean endlessly pumping out repetitions with a 1-pound dumbbell. If the weight is too light, you won't get any results: Muscles get stronger only when they're forced to use more fibers to meet heavier resistance. But Westcott's research suggests that runners should probably be working with weights that allow them to perform movements about 12 to 15 times, or reps.

So go ahead and lift, but do it correctly. Here are some common questions and answers that can help you do it right:

How often should I lift?

Most runners can benefit from weight lifting two to three times a week. If you start doing four-day-a-week *split routines,* you're going to put on more muscle. If that's your goal, great. But remember, it's a fine balance: Strong muscles are important to running. Big muscles, meaning more total body weight, can slow you down.

Should I work the entire body?

Yes. Most experts recommend a program of resistance exercises for both the lower and upper body, as well as the trunk muscles. One recent convert to full-body training is former New York City and Boston marathon winner Alberto Salazar, who now lifts two to three times a week on a multistation gym in his basement. Salazar does a number of exercises for the legs, including leg extensions, hamstring curls, exercises that work the abductors and adductors (the muscles on the inside and outside of leg, responsible for lateral motion), and calf raises. "I think it's important to do both upper and lower body," he says. "I think the extra strength will help you to recover faster from the pounding."

What kind of equipment should I use?

A combination of machines and free weights is probably best. You can start with a machine circuit if you're comfortable; but don't be afraid to wander into the free weight area of your local gym, if you join a club.

If you want to work out at home and save money, free weights may be the way to go: A multistation gym costs dough ($1,500 and up). A basic free weight setup can cost just a couple hundred dollars.

What exercises should I use? How should I perform them? How many sets should I do?

A weight-lifting workout for runners looks pretty much like those for any other athlete. All the major muscle groups need to be worked, including the legs.

The personal touch

If you want to learn how to lift properly, a personal trainer may be a good option. Look for a trainer with certification from one of the six major organizations that develop standards, teach exercise physiology and strength training, and test those who train others: American College of Sports Medicine (ACSM), the American Council on Exercise (ACE), the Aerobics and Fitness Association of America (AFAA), the National Strength and Conditioning Association (NSCA), National Academy of Sports Medicine (NASM), or the International Sport Science Association (ISSA).

A good personal trainer for runners doesn't have to be a runner, but the trainer should understand enough about running to develop a program that's right for endurance athletes, not bodybuilders. A trainer also should be able to help you balance your lifting with your running.

When choosing a personal trainer, look at the person, as well as the credentials. A good trainer is also a good teacher and motivator and someone you feel comfortable with.

Although trainers make house calls, they most commonly work at health clubs. Your local club can recommend a trainer. Remember that you'll need to join the gym as well as pay the trainer's fee, which, depending on where you live and the experience of the trainer, ranges from about $35 to $75 per hour. Keep in mind, however, that you're not signing on for life with one of these trainers. You may choose to hire one for only a few sessions. Then, after you have a routine that you know how to perform, you can get busy on your own.

Follow these general guidelines for safe, effective lifting:

- ✔ Start with basic exercises (covered later in this chapter), working all the major muscle groups.

- ✔ Perform one to two sets per exercise (doing a specific lifting exercise one time per exercise session is a *set*) and complete about 8 to 12 repetitions per set. Once you can perform 16 reps comfortably, raise the weight by 5 percent.

- ✔ Use slow, controlled movements: Spend 2 seconds on the positive, or lifting, part of the exercise and 4 seconds on the negative, or lowering, part.

Weight Training Regimen for Runners

We think that the following exercises are great for runners. Wayne Westcott, Ph.D., strength consultant for the YMCA, developed this training program specifically for runners. But versions of these exercises, which use dumbbells, can also be performed on weight training machines.

Squats

Squats are considered the single, best exercise for the lower body: Grasp the dumbbells by using an underhand grip and stand erect with your feet about hip-width apart and parallel to each other. Position the dumbbells with your palms facing the outside surfaces of your thighs. Keep your head up, your shoulders back, and your back straight (see Figure 17-1). Keep your weight on your feet throughout. Slowly squat down until your thighs are parallel to the floor. (Inhale as you descend.) Begin your upward movement by slowly straightening your knees and hips.

Figure 17-1:
Squats are great for strengthening the lower body.

Bench press

A lot of guys spend entirely too much time doing this exercise in the gym, but it does have great value in strengthening the chest, shoulders, and triceps. You can use dumbbells, as well as barbells. Lie face up on a flat bench, with knees flexed, feet flat on the floor, as shown in Figure 17-2.

Figure 17-2:
The bench press works the chest, shoulders, and triceps.

Make sure that you keep your head, shoulders, and buttocks on the bench throughout the exercise. Grasp the dumbbells so that your palms face away, and push upward until your arms are fully extended above your chest. Slowly lower the dumbbells in unison to the outsides of the chest. Then press the dumbbells upwards in unison until your arms are fully extended.

Lateral raises

Grasp the dumbbells so that your palms are facing the outside of your thighs and your elbows are slightly flexed. Stand erect with your feet hip-width apart. Slowly lift the dumbbells upward in unison until they are level with your shoulders and your arms are parallel to the floor. Slowly lower the dumbbells in unison to the starting position and repeat (see Figure 17-3).

Figure 17-3: Lateral raises are another good exercise for the arms and shoulders.

Shrugs

This movement is performed from a standing position, with your feet hip-width apart. Grasp the dumbbells with an overhand grip, arms at your side and fully extended, as shown in Figure 17-4. Keep your arms straight throughout the movement. Lift the shoulders as high as possible, in an exaggerated shrugging motion. Slowly lower the dumbbells.

Figure 17-4:
Use
shrugs to
strengthen
your neck
and
shoulders.

Biceps curl

Curls can be done standing, sitting, or leaning over a special bench. The standing curl — the recommended beginner form of the exercise — is done as follows: Grasp the dumbbells with your palms facing the outside of thighs and your arms straight. Ensure that your upper arms remain perpendicular to the floor and against your sides throughout the exercise. Stand erect with your feet about hip-width apart and parallel to each other. Curl dumbbells upward in unison towards your shoulders by rotating your wrists until your palms face your chest. Then slowly lower and repeat. Figure 17-5 shows the proper technique.

Triceps extension

Hold one dumbbell with both hands and stand erect with your feet about hip-width apart. Lift the dumbbell upward until your arms are fully extended, directly above your head. Keep your upper arms perpendicular to the floor through-out the exercise. Slowly lower the dumbbell toward the base of your neck. Then lift the dumbbell until your arms are fully extended (see Figure 17-6).

Figure 17-5:
Bulk up those biceps with curls.

Figure 17-6:
This exercise works the back of your upper arms.

Back extension

Lying flat on the floor on your stomach, gently use your hands to help lift only your chest off the floor about 6 to 9 inches. Keep your hips firmly placed on the floor. Try to lower yourself without the use of your arms, using only the lumbar muscles, as shown in Figure 17-7. Your goal is to eventually get to the point that you can lift as well as lower yourself by using only the lower back muscles.

Figure 17-7:
Use this exercise to strengthen your lower back.

Trunk curl

Trunk curls are commonly called crunches — and frequently done incorrectly by guys who knock out hundreds of these in a rapid-fire manner. The correct way to do these exercises is in a slow, controlled fashion. As shown in Figure 17-8, lie on your back on a mat or carpeted floor. Flex your knees to 100 degrees, with your feet flat on the floor. Place your hands loosely behind your head to maintain a neutral neck position. Slowly raise your shoulders about 30 degrees off the floor. Slowly lower your shoulders to the floor. Repeat. As any good personal trainer will tell you, if you're doing these correctly, you won't be able to do more than 20 or so at first.

Figure 17-8:
Everyone's
favorite:
crunches.

Chapter 18

Running for Women, Kids, and Seniors

Go watch a road race and you'll see the truth of these words: No other sport is as democratic as running.

In no other sport do so many different kinds of people — different ages, different sexes, different shapes, different sizes, and different ability levels — come together to compete in the same event.

And although runners can be young or old, male or female, most of the basic principles of training still apply. Whether you're a 15-year-old boy or a 72-year-old woman, you still need to get a good pair of shoes, you still need to start gradually, and you still need to be aware of the dangers of overtraining and heat.

However, some special considerations do apply to certain groups of runners, including women, children, and seniors.

Women and Running

Once upon a time, women weren't allowed to compete in long-distance races. The restrictions were based on some harebrained theories believed at that time. For example, some people believed that women were too weak, women lacked the endurance, and women weren't tough enough. But the men in charge of track and field back then were really afraid of injuring their own sensibilities: The idea of exhausted women collapsing at the finish line seemed distasteful and unladylike to them. Probably the whole idea of women sweating offended — or perhaps terrified — them.

This sexism persisted until the 1960s, when women — most notably, a determined Syracuse University student named Kathrine Switzer and a New York housewife and nurse named Nina Kuscsik — wanted to make their mark on the sport. Switzer became the first woman to officially run the Boston Marathon (even though the race director tried to physically throw her off the course), and soon after, Kuscsik became the first women's winner of that same race.

Both of these women worked hard to champion the cause of women's running, and both have seen incredible changes in the past 30 years. Probably no change was more significant or dramatic than the first women's Olympic Marathon in 1984, held in Los Angeles and won by Joan Benoit, a plucky young woman from Maine.

Twelve years and two children later, Benoit (who now goes by her married name of Samuelson) qualified for the 1996 Olympic Trials Marathon. Now in her 40s, she continues to compete. Meanwhile, 30 years after they started in the sport, both Switzer and Kuscsik are still running for fun and fitness. And, as race director of Avon's global series of run/walk events (see Chapter 21), Switzer is still leading the charge for women's running.

So much for women's lack of endurance!

Numbers prove women are on the fast track

The real story in running in the 1990s is the rise of women participants. In increasing numbers, women of all ages are hitting the roads, realizing the benefits, and in the process, transforming the sport.

✔ For the first time in its 30-year history, *Runner's World* magazine reports that the majority of its new subscribers are women.

✔ The inaugural Rock and Roll Marathon in San Diego drew 20,000 participants in its kickoff event in 1998 — and 55 percent of the entries were women.

✔ According to the USA Track and Field Road Running Information Center, 6 of the 25 largest road races in America are now women's-only events.

However, women do need to be aware of some specific concerns before running. Mona Shangold, M.D., director of The Center for Women's Health and Sports Gynecology in Philadelphia, offers this advice on these areas:

Running and menstruation

Simply stated, menstruation should have no effect on your running schedule. In fact, Shangold notes, exercise may actually be beneficial to some problems related to menstruation and may lead to a decrease in cramps and premenstrual syndrome.

Some women who start a regular running program may find that they develop regular periods for the first time in a long time. Many obese women have irregular periods and are at increased risk of endometrial cancer as a result. With regular exercise and weight loss, periods can become more regular, which returns the risk of endometrial cancer to normal.

Shangold stresses that the benefits of exercise to a woman (or to anybody, for that matter) far outweigh the risks.

Running and amenorrhea

Amenorrhea, or the absence of periods, is common among very active, athletic women and among women who lose weight. Shangold says that any woman who develops amenorrhea should be evaluated by a gynecologist.

Running and pregnancy

At one time, obstetricians recommended rest for pregnant women. Now physicians tell most women that they will benefit from regular exercise during pregnancy. "Running may be uncomfortable for some women," says Shangold. "But for those who have uncomplicated pregnancies, running is perfectly fine." Of course, all pregnant women should check with their doctors before beginning an exercise program.

If the pregnancy is uncomplicated, you can run up until the birth of your baby. Starting a running program after your pregnancy is more a matter of time than anything else because you may find it difficult to make time to run while trying to deal with your new role as a mother. But for most women, there's no physiological reason why they can't start running soon after the delivery. (Dr. Shangold, by the way, resumed running 10 days after the cesarean delivery of her son, who is now 13 years old.)

Running with sports bras

The old-time doyennes of track and field — the ones who didn't want women running more than a quarter-mile or so — would probably faint if they looked at the current catalogs for Road Runner Sports, a major mail-order marketer of running shoes and accessories. Under the heading of "Women's Underwear," the catalog features no less than three pages of bras and briefs, modeled especially for running and ranging in price from $19 to $35.

That freedom of choice is terrific, of course, but you do have another option. You don't have to buy a special bra to run in. "Wear something that's comfortable," says Shangold. "That's all that matters. The exercise bras may be comfortable for some women, but if you have a regular bra that's comfortable to run in, fine."

Try on sports bras before you decide to buy. Also, even a sports bra that fits well might chafe you after an hour of running. Try petroleum jelly or other lubricants prior to your run to prevent irritation.

Kids and Running

Kids love to run and be active. Yet nearly half of all American children get little or no exercise, and about one in five is at least a few pounds overweight.

What gives? At what point is a toddler's instinctive love of running and movement transformed into a teenage couch potato's diet of TV, video games, and junk food?

While public health experts and educators ponder the answer to that question, parents can take a simple step to keep their children moving: Encourage your child's natural instinct to run. You can do that by making running a game, not a punishment.

Running is the sixth most popular outdoor activity among children, according to American Sports Data of Hartsdale, New York. Over 3.4 million youngsters, ages 6 to 17, run at least twice a week.

Once, running any distance over a mile was verboten for children. But now, the medical community, recognizing that the value of activity outweighs the long-term health risks of inactivity, supports the notion of children's running . . . to a point.

"It's a myth that children cannot do a 2-mile run," says physical education professor Stephen J. Virgilio of Adelphi University in Garden City, New York. "We don't want to encourage children to become fanatics about running, but we do want them to enjoy it."

To help children enjoy running, adults should encourage children to participate, to have fun, and to understand that running is not necessarily something they have to be good at. Children need to know that running is an activity that they should do simply to feel good and to help them build endurance for other sports, such as soccer.

The problem comes when children under 12 get overly competitive (or when their parents begin to push them into competition). Although some talented kids can certainly handle long-distance running, most physical education experts today recommend that most kids 12 and under should not be running distances greater than 5-K (3.1 miles).

Here's how to help start your kid on a road to a healthy, lifetime habit:

- ✔ **Play together, don't push apart:** "How much should you push your child to start running?" asks Bob Glover, who developed a highly successful kids running program for the New York Road Runners Club. "Zero. Don't push. Instead, do things with them. Go out and kick a soccer ball around together. Go out for a bike ride together. Then, if you go out to the track, you might ask your child if he or she wants to come along."

- ✔ **Recognize and reward:** Glover's organization now has a children's category in the famous Fifth Avenue Mile. Although this race attracts some of the world's top runners who compete for money, the children's division has no winners or losers. Every child who finishes gets a medal. Most of the successful peewee races in the country have a similar policy. The emphasis is on participation, not competition. (Kids will have plenty of time for competition later, if and when they choose to compete on their school's cross-country or track teams.)

- ✔ **Start slow and improve gradually:** Children should follow the same advice that adults do when they begin a running program. Start slowly. Encourage your children to take walking breaks. Teach them that running a mile or two is not a sprint. And make sure that they drink plenty of fluids.

- ✔ **Be a good role model:** A child may not listen seriously to a lecture on the values of exercise and fitness from an out-of-shape parent. The joy and the obvious physical benefits that you get from your running speaks volumes to your children. They may even become curious when they notice the enjoyment that you get from running. When they do express an interest in running, invite them along to a local race, most of which — like the Fifth Avenue Mile — have noncompetitive kids' or peewee divisions.

I started running when I was 7 years old. It was fun for me, and it didn't matter to me what place I came in. As long as I did my best, I felt like a winner. My mother encouraged that attitude. Now as a parent, I realize how right she was. I see a lot of parents pushing their kids in sports, and I think sometimes it's because they may have missed an opportunity and want to live vicariously through their child's sports. What these parents don't realize is that every kid is great no matter how far they go in sports. It's usually parents like these who take away the fun. Instead, we should teach kids to participate and enjoy running, no matter what their ability level.

Runners from ages 18 to 91 competed in the 1998 New York City Marathon. There were 124 entrants ages 18 to 19, and 146 competitors were over the age of 70.

Seniors and Running

Folks over 65 who want to start a running program should definitely get clearance from their physicians first. They also need to be more conservative in the beginning stages of their running. They may take a little longer to build up to the point where they can run a mile or two. And seniors may need to take a longer rest between workouts.

Still, the one thing that older folks shouldn't do is think that they can't run simply because they're too old. You're never too old to start, especially these days.

Senior service

Senior runners now have an organization all their own. The Fifty-Plus Fitness Association based in Palo Alto, California, sponsors regular monthly walks and runs and bike rides at various locations nationwide. It also holds lectures and seminars on exercise and aging and publishes a monthly newsletter.

You couldn't ask for a better senior runner role model than this group's executive director,

Ray Stewart. Now 71, Stewart started running over 20 years ago and still trains regularly. He ran his fastest times at age 61 — a 38:04 10-K and a 18:38 5-K, outstanding times even for someone half his age!

An annual membership in Fifty-Plus is $35. For more information, write to P.O. Box D, Stanford, CA 94309. Or you can visit the Web site at www.50plus.org.

Running through life

Yes, you can run away from heart disease. A recent study, reported in *Running & FitNews,* tracked heart disease among senior athletes over a 20-year period. The subjects in the study were ages 60 to 92, but all had continued to train and run regularly. The results? Coronary heart disease risk factors remained low for seniors who kept up their exercise regimens.

The United States has undergone a revolution in its attitude about aging, and much of the impetus for this new perspective comes from the ranks of runners. The medical community found a living laboratory for learning about how the body ages among subjects who started running at midlife and are continuing to run today, well into their 70s. Some of the subjects are scientists themselves. For example, Stanford University's Walter Bortz, an author and an expert on the aging process, runs a marathon every year. One of the key lessons that he and many of his colleagues have found from their research is that the human body is more or less a use-it-or-lose-it machine.

In other words, if you become inactive, stop using your muscles, stop challenging your heart and lungs and blood vessels to work, then those organs may stop working at full capacity. But if you continue to exercise — your mind as well as your body, by the way — then you may continue to function far longer than previously believed. Active individuals not only have the potential to live longer, but to live better and to make the senior years active, healthy years. Running and exercise can produce such results as people age.

Where's the proof? It's there in the labs, but more importantly, it's out there on the roads, as well. Look at the 70- and 80-year-olds running marathons and doing triathlons. Look at Robert McKeague of Villa Park, Illinois, who, at age 72, finished the Hawaii Ironman Triathlon, which consists of a 2.4-mile swim, a 112-mile bike ride, and a 26.2-mile marathon run. Look at John McManus of Sunnyside, New York, who has set 25 national age group records and, at age 74, is still capable of running sub-7-minute miles. Look at the late Dr. Paul Spangler, who practiced what he preached, running marathons well into his 80s and 90s. And finally, look at U.S. Senator John Glenn, who returned to space 35 years after his first flight. Glenn was running as part of his training way back during the Project Mercury days of the early 1960s. Look how far running has taken him!

A Prescription for Life-Long Running

Do you want to continue running into your eighth and ninth decades? Here are seven tips on how to do it, culled from various experts on exercise and aging and many top senior runners.

✔ **Stay consistent:** The research shows that seniors who stick with their exercise regimen keep their heart disease risks at a minimum. You have to make exercise a habit.

✔ **Quality, not quantity, is what counts:** "To keep performing at your optimal level, you need a combination of quality training and effective recovery," says Trevor Smith, editor of *Running & FitNews,* and a runner in his 60s. "You might want to run long every two or three weeks to hang on to endurance and include some kind of speedwork once every week or two. Make sure you recover properly by having rest days, walking days, or slowing down your recovery jogging pace."

✔ **Pump iron:** As you age, you lose muscle mass. A famous study done in the 1970s by senior exercise expert Michael Pollock found that even top masters runners (people over 40) were still losing an average of a pound of muscle a year in their upper bodies. Their hearts and lungs were strong, but their muscles were weak. What's the remedy? Try weight training two or three times a week. (Check out Chapter 17 for more information.)

✔ **Get off the roads occasionally:** The collective impact of years of pounding on the local sidewalk and roads can take a toll. Physical therapist David Balsley, a top ultradistance marathon runner, recommends that runners seek alternatives: Try to regularly run on a treadmill, a track, trails, or other soft surfaces to give your legs a break.

✔ **Don't be afraid to take a day off:** Consistency is one thing. Obsessive training is another. As Trevor Smith notes, recovery time is critical as you age. That means that you need to take days off from running and perform some regular cross-training. (Turn to Chapter 16 for guidance on cross-training.)

✔ **Pamper your body:** We all lose some flexibility as we age. The impact forces of running compound this decline in flexibility. To keep the muscles supple, stretch, take a yoga class, or get a massage regularly.

✔ **Practice good running form:** Balance is a key issue for seniors. Strengthening the core muscles of the trunk and legs will help in this area, but so will proper running form.

One last key to a successful running program is to start setting goals from the very beginning of your program. "I think this is really important," says

Ray Stewart, executive director of the Fifty-Plus Fitness Association. "Even if you can only jog 2 minutes to start. Having realized that simple goal increases your confidence level."

Goal-setting also leads to greater and more ambitious challenges down the road. Maybe you want to race overseas. Maybe you'd like to compete in a marathon or half-marathon. Maybe you want to improve your time. Although everyone slows down somewhat during aging, setting goals and challenging yourself keep you fresh and interested in the sport.

And while you're at it, remember that running is more than finish times or lowered cholesterol counts. Running is about being outdoors in the company of friends or in blessed solitude, having fun, staying on the move, and always, always looking ahead.

Good luck . . . and long may you run!

Part V
The Part of Tens

©RICHTENNANT

"I used to think, 'running for the endorphins' was a charity race for an endangered sea mammal."

In this part . . .

Every ...*For Dummies* book ends with top-ten lists, and ours is no exception. We give you lists of beautiful, scenic races, great races for women only, and marathons that first-timers will enjoy. We also offer more than ten tidbits of advice that will help you stay mentally sharp as you train.

Chapter 19

More Than Ten Ways to Sharpen Your Mental Edge

Contrary to popular belief, the toughest distance in running is not the final 6 miles of the marathon or the gun lap of a mile race on the track. The toughest distance in running is, in fact, the distance from your living room couch to the front door. (If you must pass through the kitchen and a well-stocked refrigerator en route to the door, then you may even have a harder time getting out the door.)

Obviously, dragging yourself to the door for a run is more of a mental leap than a physical one. You're probably not asking yourself, "Could I physically get off the couch, tie on a pair of running shoes, walk out the door and down the drive and run?" More than likely, you're asking, "Why should I?"

After you've addressed the "why should I" question, you've already budged the boulder — ever so slightly. And after you've done that, well, there's no telling how much momentum the boulder might pick up and where such a wonderfully adventuresome avalanche might take you.

Remember Who You Are

A runner is someone who runs. It's that simple. Your speed, distance, and frequency of exercise are all only details. A T-shirt with a quote from Dr. George Sheehan (a famous running author and former *Runner's World* magazine columnist) on it that reads: "All of us are athletes. But some of us are training and some of us are not."

Think Long-Term

Veteran stockbrokers are fond of telling the bulk of their clients to think "long-term" about investment strategies. The same advice can apply to planning and maintaining a productive running program. Just as jumping in and out of the stock market is a questionable financial strategy, so is a start-and-quit, start-and-quit fitness plan.

To avoid the start-and-quit syndrome, plan a running program that works specifically for you. The program may be something as simple as three or four days of running per week. But you are much more likely to maintain a running program if it's realistic in terms of your lifestyle. Family and job commitments typically are at the forefront of everyone's life, so don't take on an overly demanding running regimen that leaves you short on time or energy for the other areas of your life.

If all runners (from Olympians to first-time joggers) should embrace one Golden Rule of Running, it's this: Running should invigorate and enrich your life, not become another stress.

Use running as a stress release. Instead of bolting to the bar for a stiff drink or flopping on the couch for a few mindless hours of television, go out for a run instead. A solitary run, or a run with a friend, is a great way to work out a problem.

Stay Motivated

Running isn't boring, but sitting around all day thinking about running or not running can be. Carve out a time of the day, whether it's 15 minutes or an hour, and claim it for your fitness time. The modern world — with its car phones, e-mail, and beepers — will conspire against your fitness goals. But don't give in!

Here are some tips to stay mentally motivated:

- ✔ Plan at least one scenic run per week. Pick the most beautiful course that you can find, even if it requires some extra time to get there.

- ✔ Don't trudge around the same courses over and over again. Even if you have a convenient loop that begins and ends at your doorstep, run it in reverse on occasion.

- ✔ Avoid overracing and overtraining (easier said then done!). Both can lead to "dead legs," which is a low-energy state even on easy running days. Equally dangerous results include mental staleness or burnout. (See the section on signs of overtraining in Chapter 12.)

- ✔ Lay off the watch. That is, do *not* time every single workout. At least once or twice a week, ditch your stopwatch and just go out and run at a pace that seems comfortable over an unmeasured route. Run the pace and distance that you feel like running.

- ✔ Join a running club. A running club not only offers a good source of training and racing knowledge but also provides support and a motivational boost from your fellow runners.

- ✔ Plan a weekend morning social run with other runners and then join them for a scrumptious breakfast.

- ✔ Read a book about running, cut out pictures of runners from magazines and post them on a wall, or even watch a movie that has a running theme, such as *Chariots of Fire*.

I travel a lot and have a very hectic schedule. But nothing helps me stay focused more than a good run. I run because it is my therapy for life — and it doesn't cost a dime!

Give Yourself a Break

An injury or an onslaught of running "blahs" is often the way that the body and mind plead for a long overdue break. But you can beat the breakdown blues to the punch by planning your rest periods before you are forced to take them. The time off from running can consist of a total rest or a temporary reduction of training, both in terms of intensity and daily mileage totals.

The perfect time to take a rest is right after you've finished a race that has been the major focus of your training, particularly a long event such as a half-marathon or marathon.

Remember that it's natural to feel a mental letdown in the days immediately following a marathon or another hard race that took weeks of training. Some runners put so much effort into the grand challenge — both physically and mentally — that they're naturally going to feel a bit drained.

Play the Cross-Training Card

Some runners incorporate cross-training as part of their yearly fitness plan. Others cross-train only when an injury prevents them from running.

But cross-training holds the key to mental rejuvenation after a hard race (particularly a marathon) or racing season. Cross-training can also help you maintain a basic calorie-burning, muscle-toning fitness level before launching into your next buildup for running. Staying in retrievable shape through cross-training also muffles those little voices harping in your head: "You're gonna get outta shape. . . . You're gonna get outta shape!"

So immediately following your major race for the season, don't curl up in an easy chair for two weeks. Instead, strongly consider an active rest. Try swimming, cycling, hiking, strength training, cross-country skiing — anything other than running. You'll still be working out, but you'll use different muscles and feel mentally (and physically) refreshed when you return to running as your main fitness focus.

Release Your Inner Warrior

By merely having the courage to lace on your running shoes, you are flirting with heroic endeavors, no matter how little you run or at what pace. You are a warrior in a war against a world that confronts you with mechanical convenience and idle luxury virtually on a daily basis. But nonetheless, you have chosen to be fit, and that choice can be a source of liberation. The choice of speed, route, distance, or company is up to you.

Face the Race

Most runners are fairly comfortable with their training routines, but place them on a track for a tough speed workout or on the starting line for a race, and their moods can range anywhere from apprehension to pure terror.

Instead of denying your apprehensions prior to a race or a hard training session, realize that some nervous feelings are normal. After all, a race or a challenging speed workout is something like a test. In fact, some nervous energy can actually be beneficial; a good dose of adrenaline can help spur you through the beginning stages of a race.

A good way to corral pre-race nerves is to have a regular, familiar warm-up routine. By concentrating on the tasks of the warm-up, such as the jogging and stretching, you're less likely to build the hill at the 2-mile mark into something that resembles Mount Everest.

Get an Attitude

Your mother or scout leader probably told you this, but you weren't listening: Think positively! You can see yourself as either the Titanic or as the Little Engine in a famous children's book that chugged over the mountain fueled on "I think I can . . . I think I can." It's your choice!

Go to the Movies in Your Mind

You can program your mind with positive images as well as negative ones. A pro golfing great once said that he never hit a shot in real life that he hadn't already first hit (perfectly!) in his mind. Needless to say, he didn't picture himself hooking a tee shot into a swamp.

Whether it's the Olympics or the local 5-K fun run, picture yourself running with efficiency and energy. If you're mentally running on a course that you've run before, plant as many real details and landmarks as possible in your brain. Sports psychologists call this technique mental imagery, mental rehearsal, or visualization.

Practice visualization everyday. It complements your physical training and will help you reach your goals.

When you use the mental rehearsal technique, don't plug in only the part when you whiz across the finish line, hands raised in the ecstasy and celebration of your new personal best time. (It's okay to include that scenario, of course!) Also imagine yourself running the tough sections of the race — for example, the monster hill on which you persevere, running slow but steady — so that your mind is ready for everything.

Relax to the Max: Breathin' Easy

Those minutes just before the firing of the starting gun will always get your heartbeat going; sometimes it feels like a jackhammer!

Just before your warm-up jog, consider some basic breathing techniques to help you relax. Breathe in and out — slowly and rhythmically — through your nostrils. Fill your lungs up and hold your breath for at least 3 seconds. Repeat several times. The result can be a nice calming sensation and can provide a perfect time to run through some of the mental rehearsal exercises. The breathing exercises can also be incorporated into your pre-race stretching routine, especially if you dabble in yoga poses.

Set Up for Success

You should go into every race with a goal, or a series of goals, but make sure that they are realistic and allow some room for flexibility. For example, if you have a personal best time of 24 minutes for the 5-K but you think that you are ready to break 22 minutes, consider a three-tiered goal system.

- ✔ **Doable goal:** To run fast but comfortable, use good form, and have a time close to — or slightly faster — than 24 minutes
- ✔ **A challenging goal:** To run as close as possible to a 22-minute pace for at least half the race and then try to hang in there until the finish
- ✔ **A golden goal:** To race smart, fast, and tough and take a real shot at breaking 22 minutes

The trick is to make your goals flexible enough that you have a big target to hit. Remember, it's the 100 near-misses that get the expert archer closer to the bull's-eye.

Break It Down

The longer the race, the more time you have to think. Half-marathons, marathons, and ultramarathons (races over the 26.2-mile distance) call on more brain power to get you to the finish line.

Here's a mental checklist to help you reach your goal:

✔ Congratulate yourself on the distance that you've already run and don't dwell on how far you have to go.

✔ Break the race into smaller chunks. This is also good advice for hard quality sessions or long hills that go up, level off, and then go up again. Focus on the next turn, the next tree, or the next water stop. Then pick up another target.

✔ Tune into the immediate physical tasks. Don't think, "I still have eight miles to go." Think, "Keep your head up, your arms active, and your stride smooth!"

✔ Go for "pack power." Unless you are jousting with the race leaders, the typical midpack group is your ticket to ride. You can achieve a feeling of camaraderie by joining fellow runners for drinks at the water station, joking with them, or offering words of encouragement. You'll marvel at how these tricks can help the miles melt away.

Forget the Clock

When you are attempting to hit certain times in a race or a daunting workout, you inevitably will have days when you just can't keep up with the stopwatch. It happens to elite runners, too. In fact, the top runners struggle against the clock more often because they are gunning for world records, gold medals, and big money — and pursuing such goals requires a willingness to risk an occasional failure.

Racing against Father Time is something of a losing proposition to begin with because you can't run a certain distance in nothing flat. However, time goals do provide a focus to both training and racing.

But the bottom line is this: Don't let the clock control you. If you are having a disastrous race or a bad workout, you don't need the stopwatch to remind you that things aren't going all that swift. So turn it off! Concentrate on finishing (there's pride in that!) and then regroup for a comeback in a later race.

Beat Slumps

Running magazines devote a lot of space and spend a lot of energy to tell you how to run like a thoroughbred race horse ("Run Your Best 10-K Ever!" trumpets the front cover), but what do you do when things go wrong? How do you cope with a poor performance or a series of less-than-spectacular races?

✔ If you demand a lot of yourself, chances are that you will not be happy after a bad race or even a sub-par workout. Give yourself an hour or two to stew, but then forget about it; it's history.

✔ Spend some time (but not six months!) and energy analyzing your race and/or training log. Was your off day the result of a race-day mistake (sprinting out too fast in the opening mile, for example), or was your training preparation not up to snuff?

✔ Don't define your whole self-worth by the digits on a plastic stopwatch or the place you finish in a race. It's only running, and you're only human. (Otherwise you'd have a metal key on your back that requires winding!)

✔ Focus on the comeback. It's the off days that eventually add more luster to the on days. Runners, like musicians or artists, learn from their mistakes.

✔ If you feel frustrated when trying to run a certain time over a certain distance, consider a new challenge — at least for the near future. For example, suppose that you've tried to break 24 minutes for the 5-K over and over again, but you just can't nail your goal. Why not train for a 10-K or a half-marathon? You can always come back to a 5-K at a later date and try it again.

Get outta town! That's right; sometimes a race in a different part of the country or world can pump you up for a peak experience. Consider a vacation to a favorite place and then track down a race there.

Don't Let Dropping Out Discourage You

The ultimate bad race, of course, is dropping out. But sometimes, especially due to injury or weather conditions, you may find yourself sitting on the curb or even in the medical tent. Take such an event in stride; even the elite racers sometimes find themselves in this unpleasant situation. Bill Rodgers was forced to drop out of several Boston Marathons, but he also won that prestigious event four times!

Take a World View

When all else fails, take a world view. Your sub-par performance in the local 5-K or the New York City Marathon may seem disastrous to you, but remember this: A billion people in China weren't even aware that you were running!

Don't Stay Down

Maybe the only thing more difficult than coping with a DNF (Did Not Finish) is being injured for days, weeks, or even months. When running is suddenly taken away from you, it can test your patience. Keep the following advice in mind when you're recovering from an injury:

- Don't mope! What good will it do? Use your non-running time to catch up on other things. (Hopefully, you'll be back running before you finish *War and Peace.*)

- Cross-train. Most running injuries are of a weight-bearing nature, so spinning on a stationary bike, swimming, and performing most weight lifting exercises are made for you.

- Keep a watchful eye on your diet. Because serious runners can burn up a lot of calories when training, cutting back on your food intake during downtime may be difficult. But if you gain 20 pounds, the comeback will be more difficult when you try to run again.

Chapter 20

Ten Beautiful Races

What makes a beautiful race? It's not always a personal record on a flat 5-K course. Scenic beauty counts for a lot, too. We don't claim that the races listed below are the most beautiful, but on a list of the U.S.A.'s top 100 scenic courses, they'd all make the cut, and most would be in the front of the pack.

Keep in mind that beauty never comes cheap! Race routes that score high on the scenic scale tend to climb hills or bridges or meander along coastlines that may be a bit on the breezy side. For those reasons, most scenic courses are not the place to plan your fastest race ever. Sometimes it's better to forget about the stopwatch and go for the sheer wonder of running in inspirational surroundings.

We list our selections in alphabetical order. Remember to always send a self-addressed, stamped envelope when writing for race information.

Beach to Beacon 10-K

This race takes place at Cape Elizabeth, Maine, on the first Saturday in August. Joan Benoit Samuelson, the 1984 women's Olympic Marathon champion, spearheaded the creation of this race. The route starts near Samuelson's old high school (where a statue of Joan honors her gold-medal victory) and finishes by the famous Portland Light, said to be the most-photographed lighthouse in the country.

For entry information: Peoples Heritage Bank, c/o Marketing Dept., P.O. Box 9540, Portland, ME 04112.

Big Sur International Marathon

Talk about a race that reaches for the high notes! The Big Sur Marathon tours along some of California's most breathtaking Pacific Ocean coastal vistas, while the Robert Lewis Stevenson Orchestra serenades passing runners with classical music. However, none of this beauty comes without effort: The Big Sur course has some challenging climbs, so marathon "virgins" should save this one for the future.

For entry information: Big Sur International Marathon, P.O. Box 222620, Carmel, CA 93922.

Catalina Island Marathon

This race, held in mid-March, has been called "Big Sur without paved roads." Dirt roads wind up and down spectacular hills on this southern California island that's about 20 miles out from Long Beach. Runners may be surprised to encounter small herds of bison along the route, but the shaggy-headed beasts typically respond with nothing more than a bovine stare of indifference. One of the most picturesque stretches in foot racing has to be along the ridge (20 to 23 miles into the race) that drops down to the harborside finish in Avalon. Those not ready for a tough marathon (and this one ain't easy!) can opt for 5-K and 10-K races that are held on the same day as the marathon.

For entry information: Catalina Island Marathon, California Athletic Productions, 304 Stonecliffe Aisle, Irvine, CA 92715.

Cooper River Bridge Run

Although this 10-K, staged each April, finishes in a major city — Charleston, South Carolina — it scores high on the scenic list. That's because runners are blessed with a fabulous view of the Charleston harbor (including historic Fort Sumter and the Yorktown aircraft carrier) after climbing to the top of the Cooper River Bridge. One of the South's grandest races, the event finishes in the historic section of downtown Charleston. There's also a 4-mile racewalk in conjunction with the 10-K run.

For entry information: Cooper River Bridge 10-K, 45 Courtenay Dr., Charleston, SC 29401.

Falmouth Road Race

A summer classic, this 7.1-mile race in Massachusetts is one of the most famous in the country. (And speaking of natural beauty, did we mention that Katharine Lee Bates, who penned "America the Beautiful," was a Falmouth native?) The strange distance just happens to be how far it is between two watering holes — Captain Kidd's in Woods Hole and the Brothers Four in Falmouth Heights — because the race course was originally concocted by a couple of barmen way back in 1973. The course winds along the Cape Cod coast, past the noble Nobska Lighthouse perched on a knoll at the mile mark, and does include some rolling hills and much-welcomed shady stretches in the early miles. Thousands of runners flock to Falmouth for this one, so it's wise to apply for entry months in advance.

For entry information: Falmouth Road Race, P.O. Box 732, Falmouth, MA 02541.

Garden of the Gods 10-Mile

Even in Colorado, famous for its breathtaking mountain races, the Garden of the Gods 10-Mile stands out. Nestled in the foothills of Pikes Peak on the outskirts of Colorado Springs, the Garden of the Gods allegedly earned its name when an early pioneer dubbed its blatant beauty as "fit for the Gods." The hills and altitude (the air gets thin at 7,000 feet) combine to make this a tough course. Sandstone spires that tower into the air, unusual rock formations (like Kissing Camel near the Garden's entrance), and panoramic views of the Rockies all add up to score big on the scenic scale for this June event.

For entry information: Garden of the Gods 10-Mile, P.O. Box 38235, Colorado Springs, CO 80937.

Mackinac Island 8-Mile

If you want to compete in maybe one of the best kept secrets on the American race scene, you've got to take a ferry boat (or plane) just to get to the Mackinac (pronounced mack-in-naw) Island 8-Mile starting line. The race itself starts at the stately Mission Point Resort Hotel and includes three waves of runners of various speeds, followed by walkers. The course offers sweeping views of Lake Huron and passes thick stands of pine trees. No cars are allowed on the island, so breathe deep and savor the clean air. Unlike most of the races on our list, this race isn't a beast in terms of terrain: It's perfectly flat.

For entry information: Mackinac Island 8-Mile, P.O. Box 233, Flushing, MI 48433.

Mount Washington Road Race

Showman P.T. Barnum allegedly once referred to the view from the summit of Mount Washington as "the second greatest show on earth." When the top of New England's highest peak is not shrouded in clouds, the view is indeed nothing less than spectacular. The 7.6 miles of virtually all uphill racing (up the Mount Washington Auto Road) is a heart-pounder, but this classic race in New Hampshire's White Mountains always has a waiting list.

For entry information (before March 1): Mount Washington Road Race, P.O. Box 990, Newport, NH 03773.

Run Through History 10-K

If you are a history buff (especially if you have an interest in the American Civil War), then the Run Through History 10-K will be doubly attractive. The event is staged around the Antietam Battlefield in Maryland each June. The course features the natural beauty of the rolling hills of the surrounding countryside, but runners also sweep past silent cannon and Civil War monuments that honor the thousands of soldiers who gave their lives in the 1862 battle between the North and South.

For entry information: Run Through History 10-K, 17835 Pin Oak Rd., Hagerstown, MD 21740.

The New York City Marathon

Five boroughs. 30,000 runners. Two million spectators. This is one of the greatest sports spectacles in the world, and it's a race that should be experienced by every runner at least once. The beauty here is concrete and steel, but make no mistake about it, the NYC Marathon is as breathtaking in its own way as any natural vista — from the awe-inspiring start on the Verrazano Bridge, through the neighborhoods of the boroughs, to the wall-to-wall spectators on First Avenue and in Central Park. But plan ahead if you want to run this marathon, which is usually held the first Sunday in November. Hotels fill up, and "only" 30,000 runners are accepted.

For entry information: The New York Road Runners Club, 9 East 89th Street, New York, NY 10128; www.nyrrc.org.

Chapter 21
Ten Great Races for Women

- -

In This Chapter

▶ A list of races for women only

- -

*B*ack in the late 1960s, women had few opportunities to compete in road races, the bulk of which were "men only." Not only are women now allowed to race with men, but these days, distaffers have a choice to compete in a slew of women-only events.

As with our other lists of races, you'll find lots of other good races in this category, but here's a quality list of ten to begin with.

Avon Mini-Marathon

A 10-K around the rolling hills of Central Park in New York City, this race (scheduled for early June) is one of the oldest, most traditional, women-only events in the country.

For race information: New York Road Runners Club, 9 E. 89th St., New York, NY 14551.

Avon Running — Global Running Circuit

In 1998, Avon (the cosmetic giant) staged various 10-K races around the United States. The Avon Mini (listed first) is just one of the events.

For race information: www.avonrunning.com or 212-282-5350.

Alaska Run for Women 5-Mile

Need a good reason to visit America's last frontier? How about a race in Anchorage in early June? The temperatures are pleasant, and the daylight plentiful for this one.

For race information: P.O. Box 230929, Anchorage, AK 99523.

Freihofer's Run For Women 5-K

Often, the best women runners in America show up for this one, but midpackers are also treated well in this 5-K based in Albany, New York. The race is slated for late May or early June.

For race information: 233 Fourth St., Troy, NY 12180.

Idaho Women's Fitness Celebration

One of the biggest races in the country (with more than 16,000 women participants in recent years), this 5-K, staged in mid to late September in Boise, Idaho, is co-directed by former New Zealand running star Anne Audain.

For race information: 511 W. Main St., Boise, ID 83702.

Lehigh Valley Women's 5-K

This race is run in late October in the scenic Parkway in Allentown, Pennsylvania.

For race information: LVRR, P.O. Box 592, Allentown, PA 18105.

Race for the Cure

Race for the Cure, a series of races (now close to 100 events) are in every region of the country and have proved to be a major fundraiser in the fight against breast cancer. The biggest races are in New York City, Washington, D.C., Peoria, Illinois, and Portland, Oregon.

For race information: Call 1-888-603-RACE.

Revlon Run/Walk For Women

More than 20,000 participants took on this month of May 5-K staged in Century City, California, in 1998.

For race information: Davis and Associates, 1132 Ventura Blvd., Ste. 414, Studio City, CA 91604.

Tufts Health Plan For Women 10-K

Run each Columbus Day, this standout Boston race is now into its third decade. The course begins and ends on the Boston Common and skirts both sides of the Charles River.

For race information: Tufts 10-K, Conventures, Inc., One Design Center Pl., Suite 718, Boston, MA 02210.

Women's Distance Festival Series

Like Race for the Cure, the WDFS is really many different events held around the country.

For race information: Road Runners Club of America, Women's Distance Festival, 1150 S. Washington St., Alexandria, VA 22314.

Chapter 22

Ten First-Time-Friendly Marathons

. . . .

In This Chapter

▶ Marathons for the first-timers

. . . .

*W*ith 26.2-miles to cover, just finishing a marathon your first time around is challenging enough. A rookie runner can increase his or her chances for success before they even toe the line. How? By choosing the right marathon to run.

Here's some quick advice:

✔ Choose a marathon close by. That is, don't fly across three time zones before you run your first marathon. (Or if you must, get there three or four days before.)

✔ Choose a relatively flat marathon. No doubt about it, hills (especially long, steep hills) make a race more challenging. But for your first marathon, you probably don't need to make the run any harder.

✔ Cool weather is preferable to hot or humid conditions. Don't run your first marathon in Singapore.

✔ Bigger isn't always better. Although we've listed some marathons (Chicago, Marine Corps) with large fields, don't ignore the medium-sized marathons.

There are more than ten marathons fit for the novice to try, but this chapter presents a good starting list.

Bay State Marathon

The most famous marathon in Massachusetts (if not the world) is, of course, Boston. But you must first run a certain qualifying standard to run Boston. More than a few people run the Bay State Marathon — with its flat, fast two-loop course — in Tyngsboro, Massachusetts, for that very reason. This race is usually scheduled for the second weekend in October.

For race information: Bay State Marathon, 6 Proctor Rd., Townsend, MA 01469.

Chicago Marathon

Although mega-marathons aren't always the best choice for first-timers, Chicago is one of the exceptions. The race (usually held in early October) features a flat course, pacing groups (if you want some help in running an "evenly paced" race), and lots of fans along the way. Also, CARA (Chicago Area Runners Association) conducts marathon clinics in the months prior to the event. So if you live close to the Midwest's biggest city, hook up with CARA to help you prepare to take on the Marathon Monster.

For race information: Chicago Marathon, P.O. Box 10597, Chicago, IL 60610.

Fox Cities Marathon

Another mid-sized marathon (around 2,000 runners), this race runs through seven communities (from Neenah to Appleton) in Wisconsin and crosses seven bridges along the Fox River. This race takes place the last weekend in September, with the trees bursting with color.

For race information: Fox Cities Marathon, P.O. Box 1487, Appleton, WI 54915.

Marine Corps Marathon

Billed as "The People's Marathon," the Marine Corps Marathon in Washington, D.C., (and northern Virginia) is typically held the fourth Sunday in October. The race offers great scenery (the U.S. Capitol and the Jefferson Memorial) and a finish (on a hill!) at the Iwo Jima Monument. The course is relatively flat and has great crowd support.

For race information: Marine Corps Marathon, P.O. Box 188, Quantico, VA 22134-0188.

Portland Marathon

Portland, Oregon, is one of America's running hotbeds, and this marathon greatly supports that reputation. Held in late September, runners get glimpses of the picturesque Cascade Mountains (but you don't have to run up any of 'em!) and cross the St. John's Bridge late in the race.

For race information: Portland Marathon, P.O. Box 4040, Beaverton, OR 97076.

Steamtown Marathon

If you want a marathon with a hometown feel, try the Steamtown Marathon in Scranton, Pennsylvania, in early October. The event scores high marks with runners, too, more than doubling its field (from 900 in 1997 to 2,000 in 1998 for its third running). Lots of downhill in the early miles makes this a fast course, but make sure you run some downhills in training to prepare your legs (see Chapter 9).

For race information: PA Northeast Territory Visitors Bureau, 300 Penn Ave., Scranton, PA 18503.

Sutter Home Napa Valley Marathon

This beautiful course rolls through the hillside vineyards of the California wine country. Traditionally run the first weekend in March, its low-key atmosphere (with less than 2,000 runners) will appeal to those runners who don't care for the big city marathons. You'll find good places to recover, too, where lots of the local inns have hot tubs for sore legs.

For race information: Sutter Home Napa Valley Marathon, P.O. Box 4307, Napa, CA 94558-0430.

Twin Cities Marathon

The Twin Cities Marathon could be on our "most beautiful race" list, too. The race begins in Minneapolis, crosses the Mississippi River at 19 miles, and finishes near the St. Paul Cathedral and the Minnesota state capitol building. Thousands of spectators cheer on the runners over the fast course. It's a great choice for marathon first-timers.

For race information: Twin Cities Marathon, 708 First St., Ste. CR-33, Minneapolis, MN 55401.

Vermont City Marathon

Held at the end of May in Burlington, the Vermont City Marathon is one of those mid-sized marathons (around 2,000 runners) that has a ton to offer. The course is rolling, with one tough hill around 16 miles, but a scenic route and spirited musicians along the course can pump up the runners.

For race information: Vermont City Marathon, P.O. Box 152, Burlington, VT 05402.

Walt Disney World Marathon

You don't have to be goofy to run a marathon, but it helps! The Disney Marathon, staged in early January, is the way to go if you are a family man (or woman) trying to keep the rest of the brood happy while you train for (or race) 26.2 miles. Fireworks and lots of characters make this a fun jaunt for first-timers, although it can get a tad warm in the final miles if you figure to still be running for much longer than four hours.

For race information: Walt Disney World Marathon, P.O. Box 10000, Lake Buena Vista, FL 32830-1000.

Chapter 23
Ten Great Web Sites for Runners

In This Chapter

▶ Two less than a dozen great Web sites for runners

A lot of people are using the Internet these days to gather information, so we thought you might find it helpful if we recommended ten running-related Web sites for your surfing enjoyment.

Keep in mind that Web sites come and go and Web addresses can change, so don't get too riled at us if some of the following Web sites disappear by the time you read this book.

www.runnersworld.com

The leaders in the running magazine world (500,000 circulation) have a good (and always improving) Web site. *Runner's World* also links you to dozens of other great running sites.

www.jeffgalloway.com

Very few people in the sport can rival Jeff Galloway when it comes to contributing to running. Galloway's impact as an Olympic-class runner/ coach/writer/motivational speaker is huge. His Web site is perfect for beginning runners.

www.waddleon.com

John Bingham is a new and important voice for beginning runners, especially the back-of-the-pack crowd. Bingham's motto: "The miracle isn't that I finished. The miracle is that I had the courage to start." (Bingham's new book, *The Courage to Start,* is due out in 1999.) A monthly columnist for *Runner's World,* John "the Penguin" Bingham manages to be motivational and funny at the same time.

www.halhigdon.com

Hal Higdon has contributed to running magazines (like *Runner's World*) for decades and has penned dozens of books on the sport. A former world-class runner, Higdon has lots of good advice for runners of all ages and abilities.

www.rrca.org

The Road Runner's Club of America can offer you tons of information on running clubs and events around the country.

www.nyrrc.org

The New York Road Runners Club connects you to the running scene in the Big Apple and beyond. If you are visiting New York City, you can always find a weekend race listed here!

www.gssiWeb.com

The Gatorade Sport Science Institute is a cool site where you can gather some helpful nutrition and training tips.

www.newrunner.com

The people at *Runner's World* offer this special site for rookies. Check it out. You can even get your questions answered by a *Runner's World* staffer.

www.highschoolrunner.com

As the title suggests, this Web site is for the teenage runners in your family or neighborhood. They'll love the info, and the tone is geared especially for them.

www.50plus.org

A super site for the over-50 (or soon to be) runner. It provides expert medical and training advice.

Appendix
Running Clubs

● ●

A great way to find running companions is to join a running club. What follows is a list, organized by state, of the largest running clubs in the United States.

Alabama

Birmingham Track Club

Address: P.O. Box 530363
Birmingham, AL 35253
Phone: 205-640-7529
E-mail: bhamtrkclb@aol.com

Huntsville Track Club

Address: 8811 Edgehill Drive
Huntsville, AL 35802
Phone: 256-881-9077
E-mail: harold.tinsley@gte.net
WWW: www.huntsvilletrackclub.org

Port City Pacers

Address: P.O. Box 16907
Mobile, AL 36616
Phone: 334-473-7223
E-mail: info@pcpacers.org
WWW: www.pcpacers.org

Arizona

Southern Arizona RRC

Address: 4625 East Broadway
Suite 112
Tucson, AZ 85711
Phone: Eve: 520-529-6501
Day: 520-326-9383
E-mail: jirish@azstarnet.com
WWW: www.azstarnet.com/~jirish/
sar/home.html

California

Buffalo Chips Running Club

Address: 2227 Northrup Ave
Sacramento, CA 95825
Phone: 619-224-8343

Loma Linda Lopers

Address: P.O. Box 495
Loma Linda, CA 92354
Phone: Eve: 909-886-9257
Day: 909-683-0422
E-mail: rbt@discover.net
WWW: jacs.ucr.edu/lopers

LA Leggers, Inc.

Address: P.O. Box 761
Santa Monica, CA 90406-0761
Phone: 310-577-8000
Fax: 213-221-6722
E-mail: laleggers@earthlink.net
WWW: home.earthlink.net/~laleggers

Tamalpa Runners

Address: P.O. Box 701
Corte Madera, CA 94976
Phone: 415-721-3791
Fax: 415-925-9377
E-mail: cjstern@cris.com
WWW: www.tamalparunners.org

San Diego Track Club

Address: 4944 Narragansett, #4
San Diego, CA 92107
Phone: 619-224-8343

Colorado

Pikes Peak Road Runners

Address: P.O. Box 1694
Colorado Springs, CO 80901-1694
Phone: 719-590-7086
E-mail: webmaster@www.pprrun.org
WWW: www.pprrun.org

Rocky Mt. Road Runners Club

Address: 537 E. Mississippi Ave.
Denver, CO 80210

Florida

Gulf Winds Track Club

Address: Box 3447
Tallahassee, FL 32315
Phone: Eve: 850-576-0585
Day: 850-644-8868
E-mail: davidyon@worldnet.att.net
WWW: home.katzlaw.com/gwtc/

Jacksonville Track Club

Address: P.O. Box 24667
Jacksonville, FL 32241
Phone: Eve: 904-387-0528
Day: 904-384-8725
E-mail: llawless@southeast.net
WWW: jax.jaxnet.com/~llawless/
jtchome.html

Manasota Track Club, Inc.

Address: P.O. Box 5696
Sarasota, FL 34277
Phone: 941-371-5567
Fax: 941-921-5687
E-mail: mojomtc@gte.net
WWW: www.sarasota-online.com/track

Miami Runners

Address: 7920 SW 40 St.
Miami, FL 33155
Phone: 305-227-1500
Fax: 305-220-2450

Pensacola Runners Association

Address: P.O. Box 10613
Pensacola, FL 32524
Phone: 904-476-7434
Fax: 904-435-4888
E-mail: bunde@cheney.net
WWW: pensacolarunners.com

Space Coast Runners Inc.

Address: P.O. Box 2407
Melbourne, FL 32902
Phone: Eve: 407-267-7247
E-mail: matmahoney@aol.com
WWW: www.he.net/~mmahoney/scr/

West Florida "Y" Runners Club

Address: 1005 South Highland Dr.
Clearwater, FL 33756
Phone: 813-595-2586
Fax: 813-595-5829
E-mail: johnsonmll@aol.com
WWW: www.runwestflorida.com

Georgia

Atlanta Track Club

Address: 3097 E. Shadowlawn Ave., NE
Atlanta, GA 30305
Phone: Eve: 404-872-0808
Day: 404-231-9064
E-mail: wft@atlantatrackclub.org
WWW: www.atlantatrackclub.org

Illinois

Illinois Valley Striders

Address: 700 W. Main Street
Peoria, IL 61606
Phone: 309-685-3921
Fax: 309-676-RUNN
E-mail: ivsorg@mtco.com
WWW: www.ivs.org

CARA, Chicago Area Runners Association
Address: 59 E. Van Buren St., #1716
Chicago, IL 60605
E-mail: cararuns@aol.com
Phone: 312-666-9836

Indiana
Indy Runners, Inc.
Address: 6822 Stratton Square
Indianapolis, IN 46260
Phone: Eve: 317-329-7909
Day: 317-849-4990
Fax: 317-849-4278
E-mail: mkdoctor@aol.com
WWW: www.rocketboy.com/IndyRunners

Iowa
Cornbelt Running Club
Address: P.O. Box 4107
Davenport, IA 52808
Phone: Eve: 309-736-9163
Day: 319-285-7505
Fax: 319-326-9171
E-mail: swedes@ix.netcom.com
WWW: helios.augustana.edu/~cd/
cornbelt.htm

Louisiana
New Orleans Track Club
Address: P.O. Box 52003
New Orleans, LA 70152-2003
Phone: Eve: 504-468-1488
Day: 504-482-6682
Fax: 504-469-9268
E-mail: notc@runnotc.org
WWW: www.runnotc.org

Maryland
Annapolis Striders
Address: P.O. Box 187
Annapolis, MD 21404
Phone: 410-268-1165
Fax: 410-547-0699
E-mail: rbowman@ios.doi.gov
WWW: www.annapolisstriders.
home.ml.org

Baltimore Road Runners Club
Address: P.O. Box 9825
Baltimore, MD 21284
Phone: 410-281-9710
Fax: 410-298-5559
E-mail: brrc98@hotmail.com
WWW: www.brrc.com

Howard County Striders
Address: 7381 Swan Point Way
Columbia, MD 21045
Phone: 410-381-6385
E-mail: webmaster@onlinesol.com
WWW: www.onlinesol.com/online/
striders/

Montgomery County Road Runners Club
Address: P.O. Box 1703
Rockville, MD 20849
Phone: 301-353-0200

Massachusetts
Boston Athletic Association (BAA)
Address: 131 Clarendon St.
Boston, MA 02116

Central Mass Striders
Address: 183 Willard Street
Apt. 302
Leominster, MA 1453
Phone: 508-537-4930
E-mail: cmsrun@aol.com
WWW: world.std.com/~cmsweb/

Michigan
Motor City Striders
Address: 10144 Lincoln
Huntington Wds, MI 48070
Phone: 810-544-9099
Fax: 810-544-4601

Minnesota

Northern Lights Running Club

Address: 1478 Maywood St.
St. Paul, MN 55117

Mississippi

Mississippi Track Club

Address: P.O. Box 866
Clinton, MS 39060-0866
Phone: 601-856-9884
Fax: 601-856-9884
E-mail: mstrackclb@aol.com
WWW: pages.prodigy.net/eilders/
home.htm

Missouri

Mid-America Running Association

Address: 403 N. Park Dr.
Raymore, MO 64083
Phone: 816-331-4286
Fax: 816-331-9422
E-mail: wink2@concentric.net
WWW: www.concentric.net/~wink2/
mara/

St. Louis Track Club

Address: 2385 Hampton Avenue
St Louis, MO 63139
Phone: 314-781-3926
WWW: www.geocities.com/Colosseum/
Track/7908/

Nevada

Las Vegas Track Club

Address: P.O. Box 72346
Las Vegas, NV 89170
Phone: 702-594-0970
Fax: 702-360-2280
E-mail: liter50k@aol.com
WWW: www.lvtc.org

New Jersey

Jersey Shore Running Club

Address: P.O. Box 7492
Shrewsbury, NJ 7702
Phone: 908-542-9060
Fax: 908-747-5213
E-mail: bobboth@worldnet.att.net
WWW: www.jsrc.org

New York

The Greater Long Island Running Club

Address: 101-24 Dupont St.
Plainview, NY 11803
Phone: 516-349-7646
WWW: www.glirc.org

Greater Rochester Track Club

Address: 1086 West Avenue
Brockport, NY 14420
Phone: Eve: 716-637-0212
Day: 716-292-1550
WWW: www.ggw.org/grtc

New York Road Runners Club

Address: 9 East 89th Street
New York, NY 10128
Phone: 212-423-2233
Fax: 212-860-8421
E-mail: asteinfeld@nyrrc.org
WWW: www.nyrrc.org

Syracuse Chargers Track Club

Address: 213 Scott Avenue
Syracuse, NY 13224
Phone: 315-446-6285
Fax: 315-449-2222
E-mail: deoja@mailbox.syr.edu
WWW: www.cat.syr.edu/~jabbour/
running.html

North Carolina

North Carolina Roadrunners

Address: P.O. Box 97336
Raleigh, NC 27624-7336
Phone: 919-846-8021
Fax: 919-846-8021
E-mail: ncrc@sunsite.unc.edu
WWW: sunsite.unc.edu/ncrc

Ohio

Ohio River RRC

Address: 2061 Dane Lane
Bellbrook, OH 45305
Phone: Eve: 513-848-2576
Day: 513-455-7209
Fax: 513-848-4276
E-mail: orrrc@dma.org
WWW: www.dma.org/orrrc

RC of Greater Cincinnati

Address: 3150 Montego Ln. - #6
Maineville, OH 45039
Phone: 513-459-0920

Toledo Roadrunners Club

Address: P.O. Box 5656
Toledo, OH 43613
Phone: Eve: 419-534-2151
Day: 419-245-2625
Fax: 419-536-1044
E-mail: darmo@glasscity.net
WWW: www.glasscity.net/users/
darmo/trrc/trrc.htm

Oregon

Oregon Road Runners Club

Address: P.O. Box 549
Beaverton, OR 97075-0549
Phone: 503-646-7867
Fax: 503-520-0242
E-mail: orrc@teleport.com
WWW: www.teleport.com/~orrc

Pennsylvania

Bryn Mawr Running Club

Address: P.O. Box 743
Bryn Mawr, PA 19010
Phone: 610-527-5510

Harrisburg Area Road Runners

Address: 431 Springhouse Rd.
Camp Hill, PA 17011

Lehigh Valley Road Runners

Address: P.O. Box 592
Allentown, PA 18105-0592

Tennessee

Knoxville Track Club

Address: P.O. Box 967,
3530 Talahi Drive, Knoxville, TN 37919
Knoxville, TN 37901
Phone: 423-673-8020
Fax: 423-525-9878
E-mail: allanorgan@aol.com
WWW: www.ktc.org

Memphis Runners Track Club

Address: P.O. Box 17981
Memphis, TN 38187-0981
Phone: Eve: 901-388-5009
Day: 901-528-4224
E-mail: info@memphisrunners.com
WWW: www.memphisrunners.com

Nashville Striders

Address: P.O. Box 128276
Nashville, TN 37212
Phone: 615-331-0111
Fax: 615-851-2630
E-mail: fjs-assoc@msn.com

Texas

Cross Country Club of Dallas

Address: P.O. Box 820414
Dallas, TX 75382-0414
Phone: 214-855-1511
Fax: 972-952-9492
E-mail: minkman@flash.net
WWW: www.cccd.org

Houston Area Road Runners Association

Address: P.O. Box 270600
Houston, TX 77277
Phone: 281-265-3116
E-mail: jlsmith@duke-energy.com
WWW: www.harra.org

San Antonio Roadrunners

Address: P.O. Box 12474
San Antonio, TX 78212
Phone: 210-648-4729
E-mail: dshingle@flash.net
WWW: www.csos.com/sarr

Virginia

DC Road Runners

Address: P.O. Box 1352
Arlington, VA 22210
Phone: Eve: 703-486-1466
Day: 202-675-6322
E-mail: dcrrc@patriot.net
WWW: www.patriot.net/users/dcrrc/

Richmond Road Runners

Address: P.O. Box 8724
Richmond, VA 23226
Phone: 804-360-2672
Fax: 804-672-9654
E-mail: info@rrrc.org
WWW: www.rrrc.org

Tidewater Striders

Address: P.O. Box 2121
Chesapeake, VA 23327-2121
Phone: 757-421-2602
E-mail: RUNDOWNEV@aol.com
WWW: members.aol.com/striderun

Wisconsin

Badgerland Striders, Inc.

Address: 9200 W. North Avenue
Milwaukee, WI 53226
Phone: 414-679-1656
E-mail: bls@execpc.com
WWW: www.runningzone.com/bls

Running Log

Even the casual runner can benefit from keeping track of his or her progress on a training program. You can use this little log to start keeping track of how far you've run, what times you've run, your physical condition, and more.

As we discuss in Chapter 4, you can also use this log to record some of the things you think about while running. Feel free to log in your bright ideas, and maybe revisit them on later runs.

Date: _____

Location: _____

Distance: _____

Time: _____

Partner(s): _____

Weather Conditions: _____

Physical Condition/Injuries: _____

_____

Mental Observations: _____

_____

Additional Comments: _____

_____

● ●

Date: _____

Location: _____

Distance: _____

Time: _____

Partner(s): _____

Weather Conditions: _____

Physical Condition/Injuries: _____

_____

Mental Observations: _____

_____

Additional Comments: _____

_____

Date: _____

Location: _____

Distance: _____

Time: _____

Partner(s): _____

Weather Conditions: _____

Physical Condition/Injuries: _____

_____

Mental Observations: _____

_____

Additional Comments: _____

_____

● ●

Date: _____

Location: _____

Distance: _____

Time: _____

Partner(s): _____

Weather Conditions: _____

Physical Condition/Injuries: _____

_____

Mental Observations: _____

_____

Additional Comments: _____

_____

Date: _____

Location: _____

Distance: _____

Time: _____

Partner(s): _____

Weather Conditions: _____

Physical Condition/Injuries: _____

_____

Mental Observations: _____

_____

Additional Comments: _____

_____

• •

Date: _____

Location: _____

Distance: _____

Time: _____

Partner(s): _____

Weather Conditions: _____

Physical Condition/Injuries: _____

_____

Mental Observations: _____

_____

Additional Comments: _____

_____

Date: _____

Location: _____

Distance: _____

Time: _____

Partner(s): _____

Weather Conditions: _____

Physical Condition/Injuries: _____

_____

Mental Observations: _____

_____

Additional Comments: _____

_____

• •

Date: _____

Location: _____

Distance: _____

Time: _____

Partner(s): _____

Weather Conditions: _____

Physical Condition/Injuries: _____

_____

Mental Observations: _____

_____

Additional Comments: _____

_____

Date: _____

Location: _____

Distance: _____

Time: _____

Partner(s): _____

Weather Conditions: _____

Physical Condition/Injuries: _____

_____

Mental Observations: _____

_____

Additional Comments: _____

_____

• •

Date: _____

Location: _____

Distance: _____

Time: _____

Partner(s): _____

Weather Conditions: _____

Physical Condition/Injuries: _____

_____

Mental Observations: _____

_____

Additional Comments: _____

_____

Date: _____

Location: _____

Distance: _____

Time: _____

Partner(s): _____

Weather Conditions: _____

Physical Condition/Injuries: _____

_____

Mental Observations: _____

_____

Additional Comments: _____

_____

• •

Date: _____

Location: _____

Distance: _____

Time: _____

Partner(s): _____

Weather Conditions: _____

Physical Condition/Injuries: _____

_____

Mental Observations: _____

_____

Additional Comments: _____

_____

Date: _____

Location: _____

Distance: _____

Time: _____

Partner(s): _____

Weather Conditions: _____

Physical Condition/Injuries: _____

_____

Mental Observations: _____

_____

Additional Comments: _____

_____

• •

Date: _____

Location: _____

Distance: _____

Time: _____

Partner(s): _____

Weather Conditions: _____

Physical Condition/Injuries: _____

_____

Mental Observations: _____

_____

Additional Comments: _____

_____

Date: _____

Location: _____

Distance: _____

Time: _____

Partner(s): _____

Weather Conditions: _____

Physical Condition/Injuries: _____

_____

Mental Observations: _____

_____

Additional Comments: _____

_____

• •

Date: _____

Location: _____

Distance: _____

Time: _____

Partner(s): _____

Weather Conditions: _____

Physical Condition/Injuries: _____

_____

Mental Observations: _____

_____

Additional Comments: _____

_____

Date: _____

Location: _____

Distance: _____

Time: _____

Partner(s): _____

Weather Conditions: _____

Physical Condition/Injuries: _____

_____

Mental Observations: _____

_____

Additional Comments: _____

_____

• •

Date: _____

Location: _____

Distance: _____

Time: _____

Partner(s): _____

Weather Conditions: _____

Physical Condition/Injuries: _____

_____

Mental Observations: _____

_____

Additional Comments: _____

_____

Date: _____

Location: _____

Distance: _____

Time: _____

Partner(s): _____

Weather Conditions: _____

Physical Condition/Injuries: _____

_____

Mental Observations: _____

_____

Additional Comments: _____

_____

• •

Date: _____

Location: _____

Distance: _____

Time: _____

Partner(s): _____

Weather Conditions: _____

Physical Condition/Injuries: _____

_____

Mental Observations: _____

_____

Additional Comments: _____

_____

Date: _____

Location: _____

Distance: _____

Time: _____

Partner(s):_____

Weather Conditions: _____

Physical Condition/Injuries: _____

_____

Mental Observations: _____

_____

Additional Comments: _____

_____

● ●

Date: _____

Location: _____

Distance: _____

Time: _____

Partner(s): _____

Weather Conditions: _____

Physical Condition/Injuries: _____

_____

Mental Observations: _____

_____

Additional Comments: _____

_____

Date: _____

Location: _____

Distance: _____

Time: _____

Partner(s): _____

Weather Conditions: _____

Physical Condition/Injuries: _____

_____

Mental Observations: _____

_____

Additional Comments: _____

_____

• •

Date: _____

Location: _____

Distance: _____

Time: _____

Partner(s): _____

Weather Conditions: _____

Physical Condition/Injuries: _____

_____

Mental Observations: _____

_____

Additional Comments: _____

_____

Date: _____

Location: _____

Distance: _____

Time: _____

Partner(s): _____

Weather Conditions: _____

Physical Condition/Injuries: _____

_____

Mental Observations: _____

_____

Additional Comments: _____

_____

• •

Date: _____

Location: _____

Distance: _____

Time: _____

Partner(s): _____

Weather Conditions: _____

Physical Condition/Injuries: _____

_____

Mental Observations: _____

_____

Additional Comments: _____

_____

Date: _____

Location: _____

Distance: _____

Time: _____

Partner(s): _____

Weather Conditions: _____

Physical Condition/Injuries: _____

_____

Mental Observations: _____

_____

Additional Comments: _____

_____

● ●

Date: _____

Location: _____

Distance: _____

Time: _____

Partner(s): _____

Weather Conditions: _____

Physical Condition/Injuries: _____

_____

Mental Observations: _____

_____

Additional Comments: _____

_____

Date: _____

Location: _____

Distance: _____

Time: _____

Partner(s): _____

Weather Conditions: _____

Physical Condition/Injuries: _____

_____

Mental Observations: _____

_____

Additional Comments: _____

_____

• •

Date: _____

Location: _____

Distance: _____

Time: _____

Partner(s): _____

Weather Conditions: _____

Physical Condition/Injuries: _____

_____

Mental Observations: _____

_____

Additional Comments: _____

_____

Index

Discover *Dummies*™ Online!

The *Dummies* Web Site is your fun and friendly online resource for the latest information about *...For Dummies*® books on all your favorite topics. From cars to computers, wine to Windows, and investing to the Internet, we've got a shelf full of *...For Dummies* books waiting for you!

Ten Fun and Useful Things You Can Do at www.dummies.com

1. Register this book and win!
2. Find and buy the *...For Dummies* books you want online.
3. Get ten great *Dummies Tips*™ every week.
4. Chat with your favorite *...For Dummies* authors.
5. Subscribe free to *The Dummies Dispatch*™ newsletter.
6. Enter our sweepstakes and win cool stuff.
7. Send a free cartoon postcard to a friend.
8. Download free software.
9. Sample a book before you buy.
10. Talk to us. Make comments, ask questions, and get answers!

Jump online to these ten fun and useful things at
http://www.dummies.com/10useful

For other technology titles from IDG Books Worldwide, go to
www.idgbooks.com

Not online yet? It's easy to get started with *The Internet For Dummies*® 5th Edition, or *Dummies 101*®: *The Internet For Windows*® *98*, available at local retailers everywhere.

Find other *...For Dummies* books on these topics:
Business • Careers • Databases • Food & Beverages • Games • Gardening • Graphics • Hardware
Health & Fitness • Internet and the World Wide Web • Networking • Office Suites
Operating Systems • Personal Finance • Pets • Programming • Recreation • Sports
Spreadsheets • Teacher Resources • Test Prep • Word Processing

IDG BOOKS WORLDWIDE BOOK REGISTRATION

We want to hear from you!

Register This Book and Win!

Visit **http://my2cents.dummies.com** to register this book and tell us how you liked it!

- Get entered in our monthly prize giveaway.
- Give us feedback about this book — tell us what you like best, what you like least, or maybe what you'd like to ask the author and us to change!
- Let us know any other *...For Dummies*® topics that interest you.

Your feedback helps us determine what books to publish, tells us what coverage to add as we revise our books, and lets us know whether we're meeting your needs as a *...For Dummies* reader. You're our most valuable resource, and what you have to say is important to us!

Not on the Web yet? It's easy to get started with *Dummies 101*®: *The Internet For Windows*® *98* or *The Internet For Dummies*®, 5th Edition, at local retailers everywhere.

Or let us know what you think by sending us a letter at the following address:

...For Dummies Book Registration
Dummies Press
7260 Shadeland Station, Suite 100
Indianapolis, IN 46256-3945
Fax 317-596-5498

BESTSELLING BOOK SERIES FROM IDG